SUPER Soups Cookbook

Over 150 super soups, seriously
healthy and simple to make

SUPER Soups Cookbook

Over 150 super soups, seriously
healthy and simple to make

Edited by Gail Dixon-Smith

CHARTWELL
BOOKS, INC.

A QUINTET BOOK

Published by Chartwell Books
A Division of Book Sales, Inc.
114, Northfield Avenue
Edison, New Jersey 08837

This edition produced for sale in the U.S.A.,
its territories and dependencies only.

Copyright © 1998 Quintet Publishing Limited.
All rights reserved. No part of this publication may be
reproduced, stored in a retrieval system or transmitted
in any form or by any means, electronic, mechanical,
photocopying, recording or otherwise,
without the permission of the copyright holder.

ISBN 0-7858-0923-6

This book was designed and produced by
Quintet Publishing Limited
6 Blundell Street
London N7 9BH

Creative Director: Richard Dewing
Art Director: Lucy Parissi
Design: Tony Truscott
Project Editor: Doreen Palamartschuk
Editors: Gail Dixon-Smith and Jane Ishoran
Illustrator: Shona Cameron

Typeset in Great Britain by Central Southern Typesetters,
Eastbourne
Manufactured in Hong Kong by Regent Publishing
Services Ltd
Printed in China by Leefung-Asco Printers Ltd

Material used in this book previously appeared in:
The Great Chilli Cookbook by Gina Steer; *Gourmet Soups*
by Carole Clements; *Natural Cooking* by Elizabeth Cornish;
French Country Cooking by John Varnom; *High Fibre
Cooking* by Rosemary Moon; *Nuevo Cubano* and *Creole
Cooking* by Sue Mullin; *Spanish Cooking* by Pepita Aris;
Thai Cooking by Kurt Kahrs; *Scandinavian Cooking* by Sonia
Maxwell; *Portuguese Cooking, North African Cooking* and
Korean Cooking by Hilaire Walden; *The Noodle Cookbook*
by Kurumi Hayter; *Irish Cooking* by Ehthel Minogue;
Low-fat Vegetarian Cooking by Jenny Stacey; *Southern
Cooking* and *Cajun Cooking* by Marjie Lambert;
Caribbean Cooking by Devinia Soskia.

CONTENTS

INTRODUCTION

Soup is a universal food. The soup kettle is the great culinary melting pot and the soups in this book come from, or have been inspired by, the traditions of many nations.

The appeal of soup may well stem from its historical importance—undoubtedly it was one of the earliest forms of cooked food. Through the centuries, people needing sustenance, with little else to fill their bowls, put in pieces of bread and ladled over hot liquid. But soup as we know it is much more than that.

Historically, the evening meal was soup—*souper*, or supper as now call it, means "to take soup."

Soup is the perfect multi-purpose food. Endlessly versatile, it can be prepared from almost anything. This creative aspect makes it as satisfying for the cook as the recipients. You can also give a new life to leftovers, which provide a traditional springboard to delicious soup-making.

A spirit of improvisation is an asset in making soup. Experiment with what is abundantly available and in season—soup is a good way to make the most of a glut of zucchini from the garden or a whole tray of tomatoes reduced for quick sale at the greengrocer. With a dash of common sense and a pinch of caution, soup can be made from almost anything. Skill and confidence come with practice. Some of the most inspired soups have undoubtedly been the result of experimentation.

The recipes in this book all have a little twist—unusual combinations, a novel ingredient, a certain flair in the presentation, an exotic origin, an interesting history. At the same time, these recipes, many of which are essentially quite simple, rely on three basic principles: a preference for fresh ingredients, careful preparation, thoughtful seasoning. All the soups that require stock will taste better if it is homemade. As stock-making requires time but minimal effort, with a little planning it is easy to have available when you want it.

Many soups can be made in advance and may even improve, with reheating, after the flavors have had time to meld. Reheat soups slowly over moderate heat until the ingredients are heated through. If some ingredients, such as seafood, are susceptible to overcooking, strain the soup and return them to the pan of reheated soup just before serving. A microwave is very useful for reheating, especially for starchy soups that can easily stick together.

Serve chilled soup ice cold and hot soup steaming hot. This may seem elementary, but soup can lose its appeal if it is served lukewarm. A tureen will help soup retain its heat, and soup can often be kept warm in its container in a slow oven until you are ready to serve it. Warm or chilled bowls or serving dishes are essential.

And why not have soup for dessert? Fruit soups can be a light and novel finish to a memorable meal. There are no rigid rules. Use your imagination and go by what you enjoy.

The selection of wine with soup is really a matter of personal choice. Ultimately, your palate is the final adjudicator and you must drink what you like. Experiment with what you think you might like and what you have available.

Making soup is a creative endeavor, rewarding for both the cook and the recipients. The wisps of steam wafting from a soup pot simmering on the stove permeate the atmosphere not just with an aroma, but also with an evocation of hearth, home, and history.

EQUIPMENT

Soup-making requires very little in the way of equipment, but you will need a large saucepan—a 5-pint capacity pan with a lid is really the minimum—or a large, deep enameled iron casserole. If you make stock often, a tall, narrow stockpot with handles is a worthwhile investment. Stainless steel or enamel is advisable to avoid discoloration with ingredients that react negatively with certain metals; aluminum is best avoided for this reason. For easy cleaning, stainless steel is excellent.

Sharp knives are essential. You should have at least a paring knife and a long wide-bladed chef's knife, as well as a good-sized chopping board or two, preferably non-porous and dishwasher-proof, and a swivel-bladed vegetable peeler. Kitchen scissors and a cleaver are also useful, as well as various long-handled spoons and kitchen string. A skimmer, a flat round utensil, perforated or with a wire-mesh insert, is used to lift off the scum or froth from stock. For this, a large slotted spoon will also do, but a skimmer makes it easier.

For stock-making and for many soups, you will need a strainer and colander. It helps to have several types: a large fine-mesh wire strainer, a nylon mesh strainer for foods that discolor, and a colander for draining.

When working with large quantities, a large 3½-pint measuring container is more useful than the usual small size. A large-capacity fat separator, also known as a degreasing pitcher, is invaluable when you need to use freshly made stock and there is no time to chill it and allow the fat to congeal for removal. This is simply a jug with the spout at the bottom so you can pour the grease-free liquid from the bottom and stop pouring when the fat on top reaches the level of the spout.

When a soup is puréed, the smoothness of the result depends on the equipment used. A food mill is handy

because it purées and strains at the same time. It consists of a rotary blade which is turned with a hand crank against a perforated disk, available with perforations of various sizes allowing more or less of the solid matter to pass through. This simple, inexpensive utensil is found in almost every European kitchen.

The food processor is probably the most widely available electrical appliance today. It produces a purée that is smooth but not homogenous and if there are seeds or fibers, the purée will need to be strained.

A blender produces the smoothest results. Because the strong suction that draws food to the blades creates a whirlpool effect, the food is homogenized in a way that the food mill or processor is incapable of producing. This is particularly advantageous in many puréed vegetable soups where a silky texture is desirable and even soups made of relatively fibrous vegetables, such as pumpkin, do not need straining after being puréed in a blender. An

electric hand blender, a tall wand with small crossed blades like a blender, produces similar results in many instances, and since it is immersed in the cooking pan, cleaning up is easier.

INGREDIENTS

Many delicious soups are made with water. It is economical and readily available, and it allows the taste of other ingredients to come through. Although stock can be an important element, there is no need to use stock if a soup has plenty of flavor without it.

The soup recipes in this book assume peeling of those vegetables which are normally peeled for cooking, such as garlic and onions, and soaking or rinsing of those vegetables that tend to be gritty, such as leeks and spinach. Carrots may be peeled or not, according to condition and personal preference, and potatoes used in soups are generally peeled except for small ones. For stock-making, peeling is not usually essential, apart from vegetables which have been waxed, but all vegetables should be thoroughly scrubbed with a brush under running water. When the rind of citrus fruits is used, unwaxed fruit is preferable; otherwise wash in warm soapy water and rinse well.

Herbs used to flavor soups and stocks are often tied tightly in a bundle to facilitate removal after cooking, This herb bundle, called a *bouquet garni*, usually contains four to six parsley stems or sprigs, three to four fresh thyme sprigs, one to two bay leaves, and sometimes a piece of leek or small leafy celery stalk, but it might also contain herbs appropriate to a particular dish, such as sage, tarragon, or dill. When preparing a large quantity of soup, make a bigger *bouquet garni*, increasing the ingredients and wrapping them in leek greens or bay leaves before securing with kitchen string.

STOCK MAKING

Stock, the foundation of many soups, is almost effortless to make. It needs more patience than skill and yields a delectable liquid ready to use as the basis for most soups.

Stock provides the foundation for many soups, as well as some sauces and stews. Ready-prepared stocks are widely available now, but they tend to be expensive. Homemade stock is easy and economical. The ingredients for stock can vary enormously, and should reflect what you have available, with some consideration given to the eventual purpose of the stock. In addition to the bones of meat or poultry or fish, aromatic vegetables, such as carrot, onion, and garlic, are essential. Other vegetables, like leeks or their greens, shallots, mushrooms, parsnips, celery, or celeriac, may also be included.

Keep in mind that strongly flavored vegetables like cabbage, kale, or turnips should be used with discretion and avoided in stocks destined for delicate soups.

Vegetarian stocks need more than just the usually aromatic vegetables to give them depth of flavor. Lettuce, cabbage, spinach, or other greens, additional herbs, and a substantial amount of the above vegetables should be used. Include some sweet ones, such as parsnips or celeriac, or a small apple or pear.

Veal bones give more flavor than beef bones. Chicken bones are more readily available, and a rich chicken

Cook's tip

Save stock ingredients in the freezer as you accumulate them: poultry giblets, necks, backs and carcasses, scraps and cooked bones from roasts, trimmings, and raw bones from poultry or meat you have boned yourself, clean vegetable trimmings such as leek greens, scallion tops, mushroom stalks, celery leaves and pithy stalks, slightly wilted herbs, or the remaining half onions when you have chopped the other half.

Store in tightly sealed plastic freezer bags or boxes. To improve the flavor of stock made from bouillon cubes or granules, add half again or twice the amount of water indicated in the instructions and simmer for about 30 minutes with aromatic vegetables and herbs. Canned chicken broth and beef consommé are useful to have on hand, but they also benefit from diluting with a little water and simmering with herbs if time permits.

stock can be used in place of meat stock in most recipes. It is best not to add salt to stock; it will be concentrated during evaporation or reduction. Season your soup, or whatever you are making, after adding stock.

PROCEDURE

Use cold water in stock-making; it helps to extract impurities and enables the ingredients to yield their flavor. The amount varies with the container used and the density of the ingredients in it, but for maximum flavor, keep the stock ingredients covered with about one inch of water, and top up with cold water if the level of the liquid falls below the solids.

When a richer flavor or deeper color is needed, brown the ingredients by roasting or sautéeing them before adding to the stockpot.

Skimming is vital. The scum or foam is impurities rising to the surface. If not removed, they will cook into the stock and it will become cloudy. Well-skimmed, slowly "brewed" stock can be remarkably clear.

Cook stock uncovered, or partially covered, and avoid boiling it. Boiling clouds stock and causes fat to be emulsified or incorporated into the liquid. If the pot is covered, the stock is likely to boil no matter how low the heat under it, and it may sour. Meat stock needs four to six hours of simmering to extract all the goodness from the ingredients, but poultry stock only requires about half this time, up to three hours. Simmer fish stock for about 30 minutes; if cooked too long, it can acquire a bitter taste.

Strain through a fine-mesh strainer as soon as it is ready. For the most limpid stock, line the strainer with damp cheesecloth. Remove the fat before using stock. Either chill to allow the fat to congeal on top and lift it off, or pour warm stock into a fat separator, or degreasing

pitcher, let it stand until the fat rises to the top, then pour off the lean stock through the spout at the bottom. You can also spoon off the fat, but this is less effective.

If the taste of your stock is insipid, reduce it to concentrate the flavor. Soups in which stock is the major element must be rich in flavor. Reduction is also used to concentrate the volume for storage. If you want completely clear stock, as for consommé, it must always be clarified. Since the clarification process removes some of the stock's original flavor, other ingredients are added to fortify it, cut into small pieces to yield flavor quickly, but the clarification itself is actually accomplished by the addition of egg whites, usually one white per quart.

Fresh stock keeps for about three days, refrigerated, and it can be boiled again and stored for a further two to three days. It can be reduced to a glaze and refrigerated, or frozen in ice cube trays, so the cubes can then be added to soups and sauces to enrich the flavor without defrosting.

STOCK RECIPES

Use the following stock recipes as a framework for stock-making. Make smaller or larger batches or vary the ingredients, if you wish, but be sure to use enough ingredients in your stock to give good flavor or it will need to be reduced to concentrate the flavor and some of the volume will be lost.

MEAT STOCK

A variety of ingredients may be used in making meat stock. Veal bones give more flavor than beef bones, but if the bones have no meat on them, it is best to add some stewing beef. You can also use a meaty cut such as shank, or add some chicken necks, backs, or carcasses to provide gelatin. Avoid lamb bones unless you want to make lamb stock.

Makes about 5 pt

6–7 lb meaty bones and meat (including veal or other bones, bones from roasts, poultry carcasses and/or poultry necks, giblets, etc)

2 large unpeeled onions, halved and root end trimmed

2 carrots, scrubbed and cut in large pieces

1 celery stalk, cut in large pieces

2 leeks, cut in large pieces

1–2 parsnips, cut in large pieces (optional)

2–4 unpeeled garlic cloves, lightly crushed

Large *bouquet garni* (parsley, thyme sprigs, celery leaves, and bay leaf)

3–4 cloves (optional)

6–8 all-spice berries (optional)

Put the bones and meat, the onions, carrots, celery, leeks, parsnips, if using, and garlic in a large stockpot or heavy pan, pushing the vegetables down between the bones. Cover with cold water by at least 2 inches and bring to a boil over medium-high heat. As the liquid heats, foam will begin to appear on the surface. As soon as it appears and until it stops surfacing, skim off the foam with a slotted spoon.

When the stock reaches boiling point, reduce the heat to low and add the *bouquet garni* and spices, if using. Simmer very slowly, uncovered, for four to five hours, skimming occasionally and topping up with cold water if the liquid level falls below the solids. Gently ladle the stock through a strainer, lined with damp cheesecloth if you wish, into a large container.

To remove the fat, chill the stock to allow it to congeal, then scrape off the fat. Gently remove any further traces of fat by wiping a paper towel lightly across the surface. If time is short, use a fat separator to remove the fat from the warm stock or spoon off the fat. Blot any remaining beads of fat with paper towels.

If you wish, reduce the stock to concentrate the flavor. Store in the refrigerator or freezer.

BROWN STOCK

Put the bones, meat, and vegetables in a large roasting pan and brown in a preheated 450°F oven for 30 to 40 minutes, turning occasionally. Transfer the ingredients to the stockpot, discarding the fat, and add the *bouquet garni*, cloves, and all-spice berries. Proceed as for Meat Stock.

CHICKEN STOCK

Chicken bones are more readily available than meat bones, so chicken stock is easier—as well as quicker—to make. If you want cooked chicken meat for your soup, use a whole boiling fowl or roasting chicken.

Makes about 4 pt

4–4½ lb raw chicken backs, necks, or raw or cooked carcasses, or whole or cut up chicken

2 large unpeeled onions, root end trimmed

3 carrots, scrubbed, cut in large pieces

1 celery stalk, cut in large pieces

1 leek, cut in large pieces

2 unpeeled garlic cloves, lightly crushed

Large *bouquet garni* (parsley, thyme, and marjoram or tarragon sprigs, and bay leaf)

Proceed as for Meat Stock, but simmer for only 2 to 3 hours. If using a whole bird or pieces, cut off the breast meat after 25 to 30 minutes and return the remainder to the stockpot.

VARIATIONS

Turkey Stock

Remove any stuffing, break or chop the carcass into pieces, and, if you wish, add sage leaves to the *bouquet garni*. Proceed as for Chicken Stock.

Game Stock

Proceed as for Chicken Stock, with or without initial browning.

FISH STOCK

Fish stock is quick and easy to make. The initial cooking of the fish parts in butter makes a richer stock, but if you wish, omit this step and combine all the ingredients in the stockpot. Avoid using the bones of oily fish, such as mackerel or salmon, for all-purpose stock.

Makes about 3 pt

1 Tbsp butter

2 lb heads, bones, and trimmings from fresh white fish

1 onion, sliced thin

1 carrot, sliced thin

1 leek, sliced thin

1 cup dry white wine

5 cups water

6–8 parsley sprigs

6–8 black peppercorns

Melt the butter in a large nonreactive pan or flameproof casserole over medium-high heat and add the fish parts. Cook for 2 to 3 minutes and add the vegetables, wine, water, parsley, and peppercorns.

Bring to a boil, skimming off any foam that rises to the top. Reduce the heat to low and simmer gently for 25 minutes. Ladle the stock through a strainer lined with cheesecloth and remove any fat.

SHELLFISH STOCK

Don't throw away the shells of crustaceans. Make this stock with the shells of shrimp, or lobster you have enjoyed for another meal.

Makes about 3 pt

½–1 lb shrimp, or lobster shells, heads, and legs

1 onion, chopped

1 small carrot, sliced

1 celery stalk, sliced

½ lemon, sliced thin

3 pt water

Bouquet garni (parsley, thyme sprigs, and leek greens)

Combine the shellfish shells and parts with the vegetables, lemon, water, and *bouquet garni* in a large pan. Bring to a boil, skimming off any foam as it rises to the top.

Reduce the heat to low and simmer, partially covered, for 25 minutes. Ladle the stock through a strainer lined with cheesecloth and remove any fat.

VEGETABLE STOCK

With vegetable stock, it is even more important to balance the proportion of water to ingredients and to give thought to the eventual use of the stock so you can select suitable ingredients.

Makes about 4 pt

1 large onion, halved and sliced thin
2 shallots, sliced thin
2 carrots, sliced thin
1 parsnip, sliced thin
1 large leek, sliced thin
1–2 turnips or ½ rutabaga, halved and sliced thin
1 potato, cut in large chunks
2–3 oz mushrooms or mushroom stalks
2–3 oz green beans or green bean trimmings (optional)
5–6 oz cabbage, or 3–4 oz other greens, such as lettuce, chard, or kale
Large *bouquet garni* (parsley, thyme and marjoram sprigs, a few rosemary or sage leaves, and 1–2 bay leaves)

Combine the ingredients in a large stockpot, add cold water to cover by at least 1 inch. Bring to a boil over medium-high heat, skimming off any foam as it rises to the top.

Reduce the heat to low and simmer gently for about 45 minutes. Ladle the stock through a strainer lined with cheesecloth and remove any fat.

SPICED VEGETABLE STOCK

This Indian-spiced stock makes a good base for curried soups or stews.

Makes about 3 pt

1 Tbsp vegetable oil
1 large onion, sliced
1 large leek, sliced
2 carrots, chopped
1 celery stalk with leaves, sliced
2 garlic cloves, peeled and crushed
1 tsp coriander seeds
3 cardamom pods
2 cloves
½ tsp each cumin seed and mustard seed
½ tsp each dried thyme and oregano
3 pt water
6–8 parsley sprigs
½ lemon (unwaxed or scrubbed), thinly sliced

Heat the oil in a large heavy pan or stockpot over medium heat. Add the onion, leek, carrots, and celery, and cook until the onion becomes softer and slightly transparent. Add the spices and dried herbs, and continue cooking for 2 to 3 minutes.

Stir in the water, parsley, and lemon, and bring to a boil. Reduce the heat to low and simmer for 30 to 40 minutes. Strain the stock and remove any fat.

GARLIC STOCK

This herb and garlic infusion is a basic vegetable stock that you can make quickly with ingredients you are likely to have on hand.

Makes about 3 pt

3 pt water
About 20 garlic cloves, unpeeled
4–6 thyme sprigs, or ½ tsp dried thyme
6 marjoram sprigs, or ½ tsp dried marjoram
Bay leaf

Combine the water, garlic, thyme, marjoram, and bay leaf in a saucepan.

Bring to a boil, reduce the heat to medium-low, and simmer, partially covered for 30 to 45 minutes then strain.

BASIC ASIAN STOCKS

For many Asian dishes, a good stock is essential for success since it is the stock that lends flavor to the dish. Basic stocks are easily prepared and soups can then be made quickly and simply. If you have no time to prepare your own, instant stocks are available from Asian food stockists.

PREMIER DASHI

Makes about 3 pt

4-inch piece dried kelp (*konbu*), wiped with a damp cloth
3 pt water
3 cups bonito flakes (*katsuo-bushi*)

First, make two or three cuts about 1 inch long in the kelp to release more flavor, then put the water and kelp into a pan and place on a low flame. Remove the kelp just before the water begins to boil.

Add the bonito flakes when the liquid comes back to a boil and turn off the heat. Leave the liquid until the flakes sink to the bottom of the pan, then strain through a cheesecloth or paper filter. Retain the bonito flakes and kelp for preparing standard *dashi*.

MISO BROTH

Makes 3 pt

1 Tbsp sesame oil
½-inch piece fresh ginger root, peeled and chopped fine
1 garlic clove, chopped fine
1 scallion, chopped fine
4 Tbsp Chinese rice wine or Japanese *sake*
3 Tbsp light soy sauce
2 Tbsp sugar
8 Tbsp red *miso* paste
2 tsp chili oil
3 pt chicken stock

Heat the oil in a pan. Add the ginger, garlic, and scallion, then fry for 30 seconds. Add the wine first, then soy sauce, sugar, *miso* paste, and chili oil, and mix together. Add the chicken stock, and bring to a boil. Remove from the heat.

DIPPING BROTH

Makes about 1½ pt

¾ cup *mirin*
2¼ cups premier dashi
¾ cup Japanese soy sauce

Put the *mirin* in a pan, and bring to a boil. Add the dashi and soy sauce and simmer for 3 to 4 minutes; then remove from the heat and chill.

Dipping broth can be stored refrigerated in a jar for 3 to 4 days.

DASHI BROTH

Makes about 3 pt

2 Tbsp *mirin*
6 cups premier dashi
Scant ½ cup Japanese soy sauce
3 Tbsp sugar

Put the *mirin* in a large pan, and bring to a boil. Add the *dashi*, soy sauce, and sugar, then simmer for about 3 to 4 minutes.

STANDARD DASHI

This recipe recycles bonito flakes and kelp used in making Premier Japanese Dashi. It is used in the same way.

Makes about 3 pt

3 pt water
Used kelp and bonito flakes from premier dashi

Put the water, kelp, and bonito flakes in a large pan. Bring to a boil over a low heat, and simmer gently for 5 minutes. Skim off any scum that forms on the surface.

Strain through a cheesecloth or a coffee filter.

SOY SAUCE BROTH

Makes 3 pt

3 pt chicken stock
2 tsp salt
4 tsp Chinese rice wine or Japanese *sake*
2 tsp shortening
4 Tbsp light soy sauce
4 tsp dark soy sauce
Ground black pepper

Put the stock, salt, wine, and shortening in a pan. Bring to a boil, and simmer for 2 to 3 minutes.

Turn off the heat, add the light and dark soy sauce, black pepper, and stir.

CHICKEN STOCK

Used to make Chinese and *Ramen* hot noodle soups and Chinese sauces.

Makes 3½–4 pt

1¼ lb chicken bones, chopped rough
¼ lb pork bones
1 small onion, cut in half
1 small leek, cut in half diagonally
2 fat garlic cloves, lightly crushed
1-inch piece ginger root, peeled and sliced
5 pt water

Wash the bones before use. Blanch the chicken and pork bones in boiling water for 2 minutes. Rinse.

Put the bones, onion, leek, garlic, ginger, and water in a pan. Bring to a boil, and simmer for 1 hour, skimming off the scum occasionally. After an hour, strain the stock through a fine mesh strainer or cheesecloth.

LIGHT CHICKEN STOCK

Used for Thai, Indonesian, Malaysian, and hot noodle dishes.

Makes about 3 pt

3¾ pt water
3 chicken drumsticks

Put the water and chicken drumsticks in a saucepan, bring to a boil, and simmer for about 40 minutes. When the meat on the drumstick shin begins to fall away, exposing the bone, the stock should be ready.

Strain through a metal strainer, and reserve the drumstick meat as a topping for a noodle dish.

HOT VEGETABLE SOUPS

ROASTED TOMATO SOUP WITH GOAT CHEESE CROUTONS

Serves 4

Roasting the tomatoes and other vegetables gives this soup added flavor, essential if using winter tomatoes.

Ingredients

2 garlic cloves, chopped fine

¼ tsp each dried thyme and marjoram

3–4 Tbsp olive oil

2 lb ripe tomatoes, cored
and sliced thick

1 medium onion, chopped

Salt and ground black pepper

1¼ cups vegetable or chicken stock

For the goat cheese croutons

4 slices baguette

3 oz firm goat cheese (slightly smaller in
diameter than the bread),
cut in 4 slices

Preheat a 375°F oven. Mix together the garlic and herbs. Drizzle a tablespoonful of the olive oil in the bottom of a large shallow baking dish. Layer the tomatoes, onions, and garlic-herb mixture in two or three layers. Drizzle each layer as you go with the olive oil and season with a little salt and pepper. Bake, uncovered, for 25 minutes, or until all the vegetables are soft.

Work the vegetables through a food mill fitted with a fine blade set over a pan. Skim off any standing oil. Add the stock or water and simmer over medium heat, stirring occasionally, for about 15 minutes, or until heated through. Taste and adjust the seasoning, if necessary.

For the goat cheese croutons, preheat the broiler. Toast the bread lightly on both sides under the broiler. Top with slices of goat cheese and broil until lightly browned.

Ladle the soup into warm shallow bowls and place a crouton in each. Serve immediately.

CREAMED MUSHROOM SOUP

Serves 6

The color of this soup resembles the pale, creamy brown of a Capucin monk's habit. It is delicious served with fresh butter and warm crusty bread.

Ingredients

5 Tbsp butter

½ cup flour

2½ pt vegetable stock

Juice of 1 lemon

¾ lb fresh mushrooms

⅔ cup heavy cream

Salt and ground black pepper, to taste

Make a velouté with 4 table-spoons of the butter, the flour, and the stock.

Combine the lemon juice and the remaining butter at medium–low heat in a frying pan large enough to hold the mushrooms.

Wash and chop the mushrooms, and then cook them in the butter and lemon until all the liquid has evaporated—the mushrooms will contribute some of their own.

Add the cooked mushrooms to the velouté and cook at a gentle simmer for a further 15 minutes. Whisk in the cream, season, and serve immediately.

Roasted Tomato Soup with Goat Cheese Croutons ▶

BUTTERNUT SQUASH SOUP

Serves 4–6

This versatile soup can be made with different kinds of squashes, including acorn and zucchini, so you can enjoy it throughout the year. The buttermilk adds a creamy, slightly tangy flavor rather than a sharp, identifiable buttermilk taste. However, if you really dislike buttermilk, you can substitute heavy cream. To save time, bake the squash the night before you plan to serve the soup.

Ingredients

2 medium butternut squash
1–2 Tbsp olive oil
3 Tbsp butter
3 cups chicken stock
2 leeks, chopped, white part only
¼ tsp white pepper
½ tsp dried oregano
½ tsp dried thyme
1 cup buttermilk
Salt, to taste

Preheat a 350°F oven. Cut the squash in half lengthwise, and brush the flesh with olive oil. Bake until tender, about 45 minutes. Let it cool slightly. Scoop out the pulp.

In a heavy pan, sauté the leeks in butter for 10 minutes. Add the squash, stock, and seasonings. Bring to a boil and simmer for 10 minutes.

In two or three batches, purée the soup in a blender or food processor. Return the soup to a medium heat and gradually bring to a boil. Add the buttermilk and heat, but do not let the soup boil. Add salt to taste.

HAM AND CORN CHOWDER

Serves 4–6

Ham and corn, such integral parts of Southern cuisine are combined in this inexpensive corn chowder. Use fresh corn if it's available, or frozen if not. The last-minute addition of scallions and red bell peppers adds crunch and color.

Ingredients

2 ham hocks

1 medium onion, peeled and quartered

2 celery stalks, cut into 3-inch pieces

2 carrots, cut into 3-inch pieces

Several sprigs of fresh parsley

1 bay leaf

3 cups chicken stock

4–5 ears corn

½ tsp cumin

⅛ tsp cayenne pepper

⅛ tsp white pepper

1 cup heavy cream

½ cup chopped scallions

½ small sweet red bell pepper, chopped

Place the ham hocks, onion, celery, carrots, parsley, and bay leaf in a large pan, and cover with water. Bring to a boil and simmer about 1½ hours. Remove the ham hocks, and cut off the meat. Return the bones to the pot, and continue reducing the stock. Cut the ham meat into slivers.

Strain the ham stock and discard the vegetables. Combine 1 cup of the ham in a large pan with 3 cups chicken stock. Bring to a boil. Add the corn, the slivered ham, and the spices, and simmer for 20 minutes. Add the cream, scallions, and red bell peppers and bring just barely to boiling point. Taste and adjust for seasoning. The ham is salty and should provide enough salt. Serve on warmed soup plates with crusty bread.

MISO RAMEN WITH CORN

Serves 4

The miso broth used in this dish has a sweet, spicy flavor. The taste of the broth will differ depending on the variety of miso used. Once you have prepared the tasty broth, this simple and quick ramen dish is ready to eat in minutes. For an easy variation, try a pat of butter dropped onto the noodles to enrich the taste.

Ingredients

1 lb ramen noodles, or 14 oz fresh or
¾ lb dried thin egg noodles

6 cups *miso* broth (see page 14)

For the topping

1 cup canned corn

A handful of alfalfa sprouts

3 scallions, chopped

½ sheet *nori* seaweed, cut in 4

Boil plenty of water in a pan. Add the noodles, and cook over a medium heat for 3 minutes. Drain, and divide into individual bowls.

Heat the *miso* broth. Pile the corn onto the noodles, then add the sprouts, scallions, and *nori*. Gently pour the *miso* broth over the top, and serve at once.

CHEESE AND ONION SOUP

Serves 4–6

Ingredients

1–2 Tbsp oil
2 medium onions, sliced
5 cups stock
2 small potatoes
1½ cups shredded Cheddar cheese
Salt
Soy sauce

Heat the oil in a large pan and gently stir-fry the onions until lightly browned. Add the stock and bring to a boil.

Meanwhile, peel the potatoes and shred them into the pan. Reduce the heat and simmer until the potatoes have cooked and soup has thickened.

Add the shredded cheese, stirring to melt. Season to taste with salt and soy sauce. Serve with whole-wheat bread and a crisp green salad.

SQUASH CHOWDER

Serves 6

Use any hard-skinned squash for this chowder. Crown Prince is delicious but acorn will work just as well, although a smoother-skinned squash will be easier to peel.

Ingredients

12 oz Crown Prince squash, diced fine
2 slices Canadian bacon, diced fine
2 Tbsp olive oil
4–5 sprigs fresh thyme
2 bay leaves
3 cups well-flavored vegetable stock
Salt and ground black pepper
1 cup white cabbage, shredded fine
$\frac{1}{3}$ cup creamed coconut, crumbled or diced
1 cup milk
1 large tomato, diced fine
1 cup frozen shrimp (optional)
Salt and ground black pepper
1 Tbsp white wine vinegar
Chopped fresh parsley, to garnish

Cook the squash and the bacon in the oil in a heavy pan for 6 to 8 minutes, until the squash is beginning to soften. Add the herbs and stock, season lightly, then bring to a boil. Reduce the heat and simmer for 10 minutes, then add the cabbage and creamed coconut, and continue cooking for a further 10 to 15 minutes.

Remove the thyme and bay leaves, then add the milk and the chopped tomato with the shrimp, if desired.

Return the chowder to a boil for 5 minutes more. Season, then add the vinegar and parsley before serving.

FRENCH ONION SOUP

Serves 6

Believe it or not, this soup is the traditional French pick-me-up for the early morning after the night before! The flavor is supposed to galvanize you back into life.

Ingredients

2 medium onions, sliced
1 Tbsp butter
2 Tbsp olive oil
2 Tbsp fine whole-wheat flour
3 cups well-flavored vegetable stock
Salt and ground black pepper
3 bay leaves
4–6 slices whole-wheat baguette
$\frac{1}{2}$ cup shredded Swiss cheese

Cook the onions in the butter and oil over high heat in a flameproof casserole dish until softened and well browned; this may take up to 10 minutes.

Stir the flour into the onions and then cook gently for 1 to 2 minutes. Remove from the heat and gradually add the stock stirring all the time, then season lightly, and add the bay leaves. Return the casserole dish to the heat and bring the soup gradually to a boil, then cover, and simmer for 45 minutes. The soup should be a rich, dark brown color.

Preheat the broiler. Remove the bay leaves and season the soup to taste. Drop the slices of bread into the soup, one per serving, then scatter the cheese over the bread. Cook under the hot broiler until the cheese has melted and is bubbling. Serve immediately, with one slice of bread in each portion.

CREAM OF WATERCRESS SOUP

Serves 4

Watercress is a tasty, peppery green that often grows wild. It brings a wonderful flavor to this rich cream soup.

Ingredients

½ stick butter
1½ cups chopped onions
½ cup chopped scallions
3 bunches watercress
4 potatoes, peeled, cooked, and diced
3 cups chicken stock
1 tsp lemon juice
2 tsp dried dill, or 1 Tbsp fresh
¼ tsp white pepper
½ tsp paprika
1 cup heavy cream
Salt, to taste

Melt the butter in heavy pan. Sauté the onions and scallions over low heat until light gold, 20 to 25 minutes.

Meanwhile, clean the watercress. Immerse in at least two baths of clean water and rinse well. Remove the leaves and tender stems, and discard the tough stems.

Add the watercress to the onions and sauté for 5 minutes. Add the potato, 1 cup of chicken stock, the lemon juice, and dill. Simmer for 5 minutes. Let cool slightly. Purée in batches in a blender or food processor.

Pour the purée back into the pan. Add the remaining chicken stock, pepper, and paprika. Bring to a boil. Add the cream. Warm until just barely at boiling point. Taste, and add salt if needed.

Buckwheat and Mushroom Soup

Serves 6

Buckwheat has a strong, slightly sweet, and fragrantly nutty flavor. It is often the principal ingredient of simple rustic soups and stews, but in this more luxurious recipe, it blends with fresh and dried mushrooms to produce a very creamy soup. Only a little buckwheat is required to achieve a subtle flavoring.

Ingredients

1 oz dried cep mushrooms

Generous 1 cup sherry

1 Tbsp butter

1 Tbsp olive oil

1 onion, chopped fine

2 celery stalks, chopped fine

2 slices Canadian bacon, chopped fine

9 oz mushrooms, chopped rough

2 plump garlic cloves, sliced fine

1¾ oz raw buckwheat groats

5 cups well-flavored vegetable stock

Salt and ground black pepper

Grated fresh nutmeg

½ pt milk

Cream and paprika, to garnish

Soak the ceps in the sherry for at least 30 minutes before starting the soup. Heat the butter and the oil together, then add the onion, celery, and bacon, and cook slowly for about 5 minutes, until the vegetables have softened but not browned.

Add the chopped mushrooms and garlic and cook slowly for a further 2 to 3 minutes, until the juices start to run from the mushrooms. Add the ceps and the sherry, then stir in the buckwheat, and pour in the stock.

Bring the soup slowly to a boil, stirring up any sediment from the bottom of the pan. Season lightly with the salt, pepper, and grated nutmeg then cover the pan and gently simmer the soup for 40 minutes.

Allow the soup to cool slightly then purée until smooth in a blender or food processor. Rinse the pan and return the soup to it with the milk. Reheat gently then season to taste. Garnish with a swirl of cream and a little paprika before serving in warmed soup bowls with warm crusty bread.

PARSNIP AND APPLE SOUP

Serves 4–6

Curried parsnip is one of the new generation of classic soups. Add a cooking apple to the mixture if you like—its sharpness gives a real punch to the flavor of the soup.

Ingredients

1 onion, chopped
1 Tbsp sunflower oil
1 tsp mild curry powder
1 lb parsnips, chopped
1 cooking apple, peeled, cored, and sliced
5 cups well-flavored vegetable stock
Salt and ground black pepper
Juice of ½ lemon
Chopped fresh parsley or cilantro, to garnish

Cook the onion in the oil for 4 to 5 minutes until soft, then stir in the curry powder with the parsnips. Cook for a further 2 to 3 minutes before adding the apple and stock. Bring to a boil, then simmer for 30 minutes or until the parsnip is soft.

Allow the soup to cool slightly, then purée until smooth in a blender or food processor. Rinse the pan and return the soup to it, adding sufficient water to thin the soup if necessary. Reheat gently, then season to taste with salt and pepper. Add the lemon juice just before serving and garnish with parsley or cilantro.

THICK CARROT SOUP CRECY STYLE

Serves 6

Anything de Crécy *denotes the presence of carrots, for Crécy town in northern France is famous for its carrots.*

Ingredients

4 oz lean unsmoked bacon
1 medium onion
2¼ lb carrots
4 pt stock
½ cup heavy cream
Salt and pepper, to taste

Dice the bacon and the onion and sweat both together over low heat for about 10 minutes. As the bacon and onions are cooking, slice the carrots finely.

Add the carrots to the mixture, cover, and cook for a further 10 minutes at the same low heat.

Add the stock, cover, and simmer slowly for 1 hour.

Press the mixture through a fine strainer or liquidize, then return to the heat. Whisk in the cream, season, and serve immediately.

Parsnip and Apple Soup ▶

GARDEN VEGETABLE CHOWDER

Serves 6–8

The crispy onion garnish gives a pleasant contrast to the creaminess of the soup, but it is equally good topped with shredded Cheddar cheese.

Ingredients

2 Tbsp butter

1 onion, chopped

1 shallot, chopped

1 leek, split lengthwise and sliced thin

1–2 garlic cloves, minced

3 Tbsp flour

3 carrots, halved lengthwise and sliced thin

½ small celery root, diced fine, or 2 celery stalks, sliced fine

2 small turnips, diced fine

2 large baking potatoes, diced

3 cups vegetable or light chicken stock

Bouquet garni (thyme and marjoram sprigs, parsley, and bay leaf)

Salt and white pepper

1 cup chopped green beans

Kernels cut from 2 ears of corn

1⅔ cups milk

¾ cup heavy cream

Crispy fried onions (see page 190)

Melt the butter in a large heavy pan over medium heat. Add the onion, shallot, leek, and garlic. Cook until the vegetables start to soften, about 5 minutes, stirring frequently. Stir in the flour and cook for 2 minutes. Add the carrots, celery root or celery, turnips, potatoes, and stock, stirring and scraping the bottom of the pan.

Bring to a boil, stirring frequently. Add the *bouquet garni* and season with salt and pepper. Reduce the heat to medium-low and simmer, stirring occasionally, until the vegetables are almost tender, about 20 minutes.

Stir in the beans, corn, and milk. Continue cooking until the beans are tender, about 10 minutes. Stir in the cream, adjust the seasoning and heat through. Remove the *bouquet garni*. Ladle into warm bowls and garnish with crispy fried onions.

GREEN SOUP

Serves 4

This soup comes from Portugal where it is called Caldo Verde. *The secret of a good* caldo verde *is to shred the leaves extremely finely. As it is so much a part of everyday life in Portugal, market stalls sell large bags of ready-sliced* couve gallega. *With good bread it makes a substantial main course in its own right, but in Portugal it is often served as an appetizer. It keeps well and is just as nice, if not better, reheated.*

Ingredients

2¼ lb potatoes, cut into smallish pieces if large

2 garlic cloves, chopped coarse

3½ pt light chicken stock or water

1 lb spring cabbage or Savoy cabbage

8 oz chorizo sausage, sliced (optional)

Salt and ground black pepper

4–6 Tbsp olive oil, to serve

1 Tbsp cilantro leaves, to serve (optional)

Put the potatoes, garlic, and stock or water into a large pan, bring to a boil, and simmer gently for 15 minutes, or until tender.

Meanwhile, remove the stems from the cabbage leaves. Roll the leaves into tubes and then cut across them to shred as thinly as possible.

Mash the potatoes and garlic together in the saucepan to form a fairly smooth purée. Add the cabbage and sausage, if using, and simmer for about 5 minutes, until warmed through. Season to taste.

Ladle into warmed soup bowls and swirl some olive oil into each portion. Scatter over a few cilantro leaves, if using, and serve.

BUTTERNUT AND ORANGE SOUP

Serves 4–6

This soup has South African origins. It is a wonderful combination of flavors and will quickly establish itself as a family favorite. Do not boil the soup after adding the orange juice or the flavor will become slightly tainted.

Ingredients

1 onion, chopped
2 Tbsp vegetable oil
1–2 butternut squashes, weighing about 2 lb, peeled and diced
Shredded rind and juice of 2 oranges
2¾ pt well-flavored vegetable stock
2 bay leaves
Salt and ground black pepper
Grated fresh nutmeg
2 Tbsp parsley, chopped fresh

Cook the onion in the oil until softened but not browned, then add the prepared squash and cook slowly for 5 minutes, stirring occasionally. Stir in the grated orange rind then add the stock, bay leaves, and seasonings. Bring the soup to a boil, then cover, and simmer gently for 40 minutes, until the squash is tender and cooked through.

Allow the soup to cool slightly, remove the bay leaves, then purée in a blender or food processor until smooth. Rinse the pan and return the soup to it, adding the orange juice. Reheat the soup slowly—do not let it boil—then season to taste. Add the chopped fresh parsley just before serving piping hot.

SORREL SOUP

Serves 4

Here is a delicious French-inspired mushroom soup. The inclusion of lemon juice gives a wonderful edge to the flavor.

Ingredients

½ stick butter
1 large Spanish onion
4 garlic cloves
1 lb sorrel
4 pt chicken stock
2 Tbsp medium oatmeal
Salt and pepper
⅔ cup lightly whipped cream

Melt the butter. Chop the onion and the garlic and soften them in the butter. Wash and tear the sorrel, and melt it in the butter and onions. Add the stock and bring to a boil.

Scatter in the oatmeal and stir until cooked. Season to taste, and simmer for 1 hour. Serve in warm bowls with a dollop of whipped cream.

SESAME, CARROT, AND PARSNIP SOUP

Serves 4–6

Ingredients

1 Tbsp butter
1 onion, chopped
1 leek, split and sliced
1 lb carrots, sliced
2 medium parsnips, peeled and sliced
1–2 garlic cloves, minced
3 cups water
7–8 coriander seeds
1–2 cardamom pods
½ tsp fresh thyme leaves, or a pinch of dried thyme
Salt and ground black pepper
Zest of ½ orange (unwaxed or scrubbed)
¼ tsp oriental sesame oil, or to taste
3 cups chicken or vegetable stock

For the sesame croutons

3 thin slices white or whole-wheat bread, crust removed
Soft butter, for spreading
2 Tbsp sesame seeds

Melt the butter in a pan over medium heat and add the onion and leek. Cook until soft, about 5 minutes, stirring occasionally. Add the carrots, parsnips, garlic, and water. Tie the spices and thyme in a piece of cheesecloth and add to the soup with salt and pepper. Bring to a boil, reduce the heat to low, and simmer gently, partially covered, until the vegetables are tender, about 45 minutes.

Transfer the vegetables and cooking liquid to a blender fitted with a steel blade and purée until smooth. Return to the pan, add the orange zest, sesame oil, and stock, and simmer over very low heat, stirring occasionally.

For the croutons, preheat a 375°F oven. Spread the bread lightly with butter, sprinkle with sesame seeds, and lightly press them into the butter to help them to adhere. Cut each piece of bread diagonally into four triangles, then cut each triangle in half to form two smaller triangles. Bake until golden and crispy, about 15 minutes.

Ladle the soup into warmed bowls and top with croutons.

MINTED PEA SOUP

Serves 6

Pea Soup is one of the great classics. Use frozen peas and just add a little lime for an extra brightness of flavor. The essential ingredients are young peas and fresh mint. This soup is just as good hot or served cold over crushed ice in the summer.

Ingredients

1 small onion, chopped fine
2 Tbsp butter
1 lb frozen peas
2 Tbsp chopped fresh mint
5 cups water
Shredded rind of 1 lime
Salt and white pepper, to taste
Light cream, to serve

Cook the onion slowly in the butter until soft but not brown; it is important to soften the onion really well as this soup has a very short cooking time. Stir in the peas and the mint, then add the water, and bring the soup to a boil. Simmer for only 3 to 4 minutes, until the peas are just cooked—this will preserve the bright color of the soup.

Cool the soup slightly then add the lime rind and purée until smooth in a blender. Rinse the pan and return the soup to it, seasoning to taste with salt and white pepper. Reheat gently. Serve with a swirl of light cream.

SPINACH AND ZUCCHINI SOUP

Serves 8

This soup is a dramatic dark green in color and has a strong peppery flavor.

Ingredients

1 small onion, chopped fine
1 Tbsp oil
1–2 garlic cloves, crushed
1 lb frozen leaf spinach
2 zucchini, trimmed and shredded
3 pt well-flavored vegetable stock
Salt and ground black pepper
Grated fresh nutmeg
1 Tbsp fresh basil leaves, roughly torn
Shredded zucchini and whole-wheat croutons, to garnish

Cook the onion in the oil until soft then add the garlic, spinach, and zucchini. Mix well, then stir in the stock and bring the soup to a boil. Season lightly with salt, pepper, and nutmeg then simmer the soup for 20 minutes.

Allow the soup to cool slightly, add the basil leaves, then purée until smooth in a blender or food processor.

Reheat gently, season to taste, then serve the soup garnished with raw zucchini and whole-wheat croutons.

Minted Pea Soup ▶

SUMMER VEGETABLE SOUP

Serves 6–8

Made from summer vegetables picked at their absolute peak of freshness, this is a light, healthy soup.
It is a favorite for a lunch or a late supper.

Ingredients

4 small carrots
1 small cauliflower
2 new potatoes
8 oz green beans
4 small radishes, halved
6 oz peas
4 oz fresh spinach, washed
2 Tbsp butter
2 tsp salt
2 Tbsp flour
⅓ cup milk
1 egg yolk
¼ cup heavy cream
8 oz small peeled shrimp
1 tsp white pepper
2 Tbsp chopped fine fresh dill or parsley

Prepare and cut the carrots, cauliflower, potatoes, and beans into ¼-inch cubes. Place the cubed vegetables with the radishes and peas in a pan, cover with water, and add the salt. Boil, uncovered, for 5 minutes or until tender. Add the spinach and cook for another 5 minutes. Strain the liquid into a bowl and put the vegetables into another bowl.

Melt the butter, remove from the heat and stir in the salt and flour. Slowly add the reserved hot vegetable stock, whisking all the time, then beat in the milk. Mix the egg yolk and cream in a bowl. Whisk ⅔ cup of the hot soup into the egg mixture, spooning it in. Then whisk the warmed egg and cream mixture back into the soup.

Add the vegetables to the soup and reheat. Just before it boils, add the shrimp and simmer for 3 to 4 minutes. Stir in the white pepper. Serve with chopped dill or parsley.

ASPARAGUS SOUP

Serves 6

Ingredients

½ stick butter
6 Tbsp flour
3 pt light stock
1 lb asparagus
⅔ cup heavy cream
Salt and ground black pepper

Make a light roux with the butter and flour. Slowly add the stock and bring the mixture to a boil. Turn down the heat.

Cut the heads from the asparagus and set aside. Cut away the tough, whitish bottoms and discard. Chop the remaining green parts and add to the roux and stock.

Simmer the mixture for 50 minutes, then liquidize or strain. Return the mixture to low heat.

Blanch the asparagus heads in boiling, salted water for 5 minutes.

Before serving, stir the cream into the soup and season with the salt and pepper. Serve very hot, garnished with the asparagus heads.

◀ *Summer Vegetable Soup*

GREEN "PISTOU" SOUP

Serves 4

The lovely, all-green color is an unexpected delight—add pasta if you like. To make a classic pistou add a handful of cooked vermicelli, broken into the pot.

Ingredients

1 leek, chopped
2 onions, chopped
5 garlic cloves, chopped coarse
3 Tbsp extra virgin olive oil
3 medium-sized ripe, yellow tomatoes, diced
Salt and ground black pepper
A pinch of sugar
3½ cups vegetable stock
3½ cups water
3 small zucchini, cut into bite-sized pieces
1 medium-sized potato, peeled and diced
¼ cabbage, sliced thin
¾ cup fresh, white, shell beans, such as cooked cannellini
8 chard or spinach leaves, sliced thin
¼–½ bunch broccoli, cut into florets
A handful of green beans, cut into bite-sized pieces
1 quantity of pistou (see page 39)
Extra grated Parmesan cheese, to serve

Lightly sauté the leek, onion, and garlic in the olive oil until they are soft, then add the tomatoes, seasoning, and sugar, and cook over a medium heat about 10 minutes. Add the vegetable stock and water, the zucchini, potato, and cabbage, and continue to cook over medium heat until the potatoes are just tender and the zucchini are quite soft. The cabbage will be soft by now, too.

Add the white beans, chard or spinach leaves, broccoli, and green beans, and cook for about another 5 minutes, or until the broccoli and green beans are cooked through.

Serve immediately in warmed bowls with a tablespoon or two of pistou stirred in, accompanied by the grated Parmesan sprinkled on top. Do not heat the pistou, or its fragrance will quickly dissipate.

PISTOU

Serves 4

Unlike pesto, this pounded paste of basil, garlic, and olive oil does not have a thickening made with crushed nuts, but like pesto, it is often enriched with shredded, sharp, Parmesan cheese. Pistou flavors vary, between using more or less garlic for pungency, extra basil for freshness and fragrance, and olive oil for a smooth, rich texture.

Ingredients

3 garlic cloves, peeled

Several handfuls of fresh, basil leaves, torn coarsely

5 Tbsp extra virgin olive oil, or more as needed

6 Tbsp shredded Parmesan cheese, to taste

Crush the garlic cloves with a mortar and pestle, then transfer to a food processor or blender, and continue crushing. Add the basil, then slowly add the olive oil, working the mixture in until it forms a smooth paste. Add enough olive oil for it to be smooth and oily, then stir in the cheese.

Store the pistou in a covered bowl or jar with a layer of olive oil over the top, for no longer than two days in a refrigerator. If you should wish to store the pistou longer, you can freeze it for up to four months, but be certain to omit the cheese when freezing to ensure freshness.

CARROT-TURNIP SOUP

Serves 4

Carrot and turnip are simmered in chicken stock, puréed into a thick broth, then seasoned with orange juice and ginger.

Ingredients

1½ cups chopped onion

2 Tbsp olive oil or butter

1½ lb carrots, peeled and chopped fine

1 medium turnip, peeled and chopped

4 cups chicken stock

¼ cup orange juice

1 tsp ground ginger

¼ tsp nutmeg

Salt and ground black pepper

Sauté the onions in oil or butter until golden, about 25 minutes. Put the onions in a pan with the carrots, turnip, and chicken stock. Bring to a boil, reduce the heat, and simmer, uncovered for 40 minutes. Purée the soup and return it to the heat. Add the orange juice, ginger, and nutmeg. Bring the mixture to a boil, then reduce the heat and simmer for 5 minutes. Taste and add salt and pepper, and adjust the ginger if desired.

VEGETABLE AND FRESH CILANTRO SOUP

Serves 4–6

A light, fresh-tasting soup that is ideal either as an appetizer or as a light lunch.

Ingredients

5 cups vegetable stock
6 oz dried pasta (any shape)
A dash of olive oil
2 medium carrots, sliced thin
1 cup frozen peas
6 Tbsp chopped fresh cilantro
Salt and ground black pepper

Bring the vegetable stock to a boil in a large pan, and add the pasta with a dash of olive oil. Cook for about 5 minutes, stirring occasionally, then add the sliced carrots.

Cook for 5 minutes, then add the peas and cilantro. Season with salt and freshly ground black pepper and simmer gently for about 10 minutes, stirring occasionally, until the pasta and carrots are tender. Serve the soup with shredded cheese, if wished.

HARVEST SOUP

Serves 4–6

Ingredients

1–2 tsp oil
1 onion, chopped fine
2¼ cups pumpkin, peeled and diced
2 cups carrots, sliced fine
2 potatoes
Juice of ½ a lemon
5 cups stock
Salt and ground black pepper
1 zucchini, sliced (optional)
⅓ cup sliced green beans (optional)
Basil leaves, to garnish

Heat the oil in a large pan and fry the onion until translucent.

Add the pumpkin, carrots, and potatoes and pour over the lemon juice. Sweat, covered, for 5 minutes.

Add the stock and seasoning and simmer until the potatoes are cooked. Blend or part-blend the soup.

If you like, add zucchini and beans and simmer for a further 4 minutes. Check the seasoning.

Serve garnished with basil leaves. This soup can also be served sprinkled with Parmesan cheese.

JERUSALEM ARTICHOKE SOUP

Serves 3–4

This native North American vegetable is used to make a silky, genteel soup typical of the Victorian era.

Ingredients

1 lemon (unwaxed or scrubbed)
1 lb Jerusalem artichokes
1 Tbsp butter
1 shallot, chopped
½ onion, chopped
3 cups chicken or veal stock
3 Tbsp heavy cream
Salt and white pepper
Borage flowers or Italian parsley, to garnish

Finely shred the zest from the lemon and set aside. Fill a medium-size bowl with cold water and then add the juice of ½ lemon.

Peel the Jerusalem artichokes and cut large ones in two or three pieces. Drop into the acidulated water to prevent discoloration.

Melt the butter in a heavy pan over medium heat. Add the shallot and onion and cook, stirring frequently, until just softened, about 4 minutes. Drain the Jerusalem artichokes and add them to the pan with the stock.

Bring just to a boil, reduce the heat, and simmer gently until the vegetables are tender, 15 to 20 minutes.

Transfer the solids to a blender or a food processor fitted with a steel blade, add some of the cooking liquid and purée until smooth. Return to the saucepan with the remaining cooking liquid, add the cream, salt, pepper, and lemon zest and juice to taste. Set over medium-low heat and simmer for 3 to 5 minutes until reheated. Ladle the soup into warm bowls and float a borage flower or parsley leaf on top.

BEET SOUP WITH HORSERADISH

Serves 6

If you think of a soup made with beet you immediately think of Borscht, the classic Russian soup.
This recipe uses cooked beet combined with white turnips and horseradish for a peppery soup.

Ingredients

1 onion, chopped fine
2 medium white turnips, diced
1 Tbsp vegetable oil
1 lb cooked beet, diced
3 pt well-flavored vegetable stock
Salt and ground black pepper
4 bay leaves
2 tsp grated horseradish
1 Tbsp fresh snipped chives
½ cup sour cream

Cook the onion and the turnip in the oil until softened but not browned, then add the beet and the stock, and bring to a boil. Reduce the heat, add the seasoning, bay leaves, and 1 teaspoon horseradish, then cover, and simmer for 30 to 40 minutes.

Allow the soup to cool slightly and remove the bay leaves. Then purée until smooth in a blender or food processor with a steel blade.

Rinse the pan and return the soup to it, then reheat the soup gently. Mix the remaining horseradish and the chives into the sour cream. Season the soup to taste then serve with a dollop of the flavored cream in each portion.

RAMEN WITH STIR-FRIED VEGETABLES

Serves 4

Ramen *noodles topped with a blend of fresh and flash-fried vegetables—deliciously simple and simply delicious!*

Ingredients

1 lb *ramen* noodles, or 14 oz fresh or ¾ lb dried thin egg noodles

6 cups soy sauce broth (see page 15)

For the topping

2 Tbsp vegetable oil

1 Tbsp sesame oil

1 small onion, sliced

¾ cup snow peas, cut in half diagonally

2–3 small carrots, cut into long matchsticks

2½ cups bean sprouts

½ lb Chinese cabbage, chopped

2 dried black ear fungi or dried *shiitake* mushrooms, soaked in water, rinsed, and chopped

Salt and ground black pepper

Heat the oils in a wok or frying pan until very hot. Stir-fry the onion, snow peas, and carrots for 2 minutes, then add the bean sprouts, Chinese cabbage, black fungi or mushrooms, and stir-fry for another 3 to 4 minutes. Season with salt and pepper to taste.

Boil plenty of water in a large pan, and add the noodles. Cook for 3 minutes before draining well. Put the noodles into four bowls.

Heat the soy sauce broth. Pile the stir-fried vegetables onto the noodles, and pour the broth over the top.

MINESTRONE SOUP

Serves 4–6

There are many versions of this classic soup; this one is simple, wholesome, and filling. Serve with warm, crusty garlic bread.

Ingredients

1 Tbsp extra virgin olive oil
3 garlic cloves, crushed
1 lb carrots, peeled and diced fine
1 lb zucchini, diced fine
3 oz dried pastina (any tiny pasta shapes)
5 Tbsp chopped fresh parsley
2 oz vegetable paste
3 pt well-flavored vegetable stock
Salt and ground black pepper
Freshly shredded Parmesan cheese, to serve

Heat the olive oil in a large pan and add the garlic. Sauté for about 2 minutes, then stir in the diced carrots and zucchini. Cook for about 5 minutes, stirring occasionally.

Stir in the pastina and chopped parsley into the vegetable mixture, add the vegetable paste and vegetable stock, and season with salt and ground black pepper.

Cover and simmer for about 30 minutes, until the vegetables and pasta have softened and the flavors have developed. Serve with freshly shredded Parmesan cheese.

BROCCOLI SOUP

Serves 6

It is hard to imagine a simpler soup than this, or one that is more delicious. The flavor of the broccoli is delicate, almost like asparagus, and using water rather than stock allows that flavor to shine through.

Ingredients

1 onion, chopped fine
1 Tbsp butter
2 large heads broccoli weighing about 1 lb in total
Salt and ground black pepper
3 cups water
1¾ cups milk
Grated fresh nutmeg
Light cream (optional)

Cook the onion in the butter until softened but not browned. Trim the broccoli and chop it roughly, using the stalks and the florets. Add the broccoli to the pan, tossing it in the hot juices, then season lightly, and add the water. Bring to a boil then simmer for 30 minutes, until the broccoli is soft.

Cool slightly, then purée the soup in a blender or food processor. Rinse the pan and return the soup to it with the milk, then heat slowly until almost at a boil. Remove from the heat; season to taste with salt, pepper, and nutmeg; then serve immediately with a swirl of cream, if you wish.

Minestrone Soup ▶

MISO RAMEN WITH SHREDDED LEEK

Serves 4

Noodles in miso broth are one of the most popular noodle dishes served in Japan. It is essential to use a good quality miso paste as this provides the crucial sweet and salty flavoring to the dish. The shredded leek should have a firm, supple texture, so if prepared beforehand, soak it in a little water to prevent it from drying out.

Ingredients

½ lb fresh spinach

1 lb *ramen* noodles, or 14 oz fresh or ¾ lb dried egg noodles

3 pt *miso* broth (see page 14)

4-inch piece of leek, cut in four pieces and shredded

4 Tbsp cooked dried bamboo shoots (*shinachiku*) (optional)

Bring some water to a boil in a pan, and blanch the spinach for 1 to 2 minutes. Rinse, drain, and divide into four equal portions.

Bring more water to a boil in a large pan. Add the noodles, and boil for 4 minutes. Drain, and divide among individual serving bowls.

Heat the *miso* broth for 2 to 3 minutes. Pile the leek, spinach, and bamboo shoots on top of the noodles. Add the *miso* broth, and serve.

CREAM OF CAULIFLOWER AND CUMIN SOUP

Serves 6

This is deliciously light flavored soup, cooked for the minimum time so that there is plenty of texture despite it being blended. Serve with a salsa of curried vegetables if you wish, but the subtly spiced flavor of the cauliflower should dominate.

Ingredients

1 tsp cumin seeds

1 medium onion, chopped fine

1 Tbsp oil

1 lb 2 oz cauliflower florets and stalks, chopped rough

1¾ cups milk

3 cups vegetable stock

Salt and ground black pepper

◄ *Miso Ramen with Shredded Leek*

Heat a frying pan until hot, then add the cumin seeds, and roast for 1 to 2 minutes. Cool slightly then grind to a fine powder in a pestle and mortar or with the end of a rolling pin.

Cook the onion in the oil until soft but not browned, then add the ground cumin and cauliflower. Continue cooking for 1 to 2 minutes, add the milk, stock, and seasonings. Bring to a boil, then simmer for just 10 minutes.

Cool slightly before blending in a blender or food processor until smooth. Rinse the pan, return the soup to it and reheat, seasoning to taste.

WHITE RADISH SOUP

Serves 4–6

This warming, soothing Korean soup is usually served for breakfast.

Ingredients

16 dried Chinese mushrooms, soaked in
hot water for 30 minutes

$3\frac{1}{2}$ pt chicken stock (see page 12)

1 lb diced white radish

10 oz mung bean sprouts

1 tsp soy sauce

$\frac{1}{2}$ tsp sugar

Ground black pepper

Remove the mushrooms from the soaking water. Drain and reserve the water.

Remove and discard the stalks from the mushrooms. Thinly slice the caps and put into a large pan with the stock. Bring to a boil and add the white radish. Cover the pan and simmer slowly for about 10 minutes until the white radish is tender.

Add the bean sprouts, return to a boil. Cover again and simmer for 3 to 4 minutes more. Add the soy sauce, sugar, and pepper.

CALLALOO

Serves 4–6

No matter what its spelling—calaloo, callilu, callau, kalalou, or callaloo—this soup is celebrated throughout the Caribbean. Its name is taken from its chief ingredient, the leaves of the tuberous taro or callaloo plant, but cooks outside the Caribbean have found that fresh spinach, Swiss chard, kale, and Indian bhaji are quite similar to callaloo and a lot easier to track down. Mint-green in color and with a subtle, sharp flavor, the soup makes a refreshing opener for any meal.

Ingredients

8 oz fresh spinach, Swiss chard, or Indian bhaji
4 oz okra, sliced (optional)
8 oz eggplant, peeled and chopped into bite-sized pieces
4 cups water
1 Tbsp vegetable oil
2 onions, chopped fine
2 garlic cloves, minced
$\frac{1}{2}$ tsp thyme
$\frac{1}{4}$ tsp allspice
2 Tbsp snipped fresh chives
1 fresh chile pepper, seeded and chopped
1 Tbsp white wine vinegar
1 cup coconut milk
Salt and ground black pepper

Wash and drain the greens, discarding the stems. Chop the leaves into pieces. Place in a large, heavy-based pan with the okra, if using, and the eggplant. Add the water and cook over medium heat until the vegetables are tender, about 15 minutes. (If you have added okra, check frequently as this vegetable tends to become glutinous if overcooked.)

Heat the oil in a heavy frying pan and sauté the onions and garlic until the onions are just translucent. Add the remaining ingredients, plus the onions and garlic, to the vegetables, and simmer for 5 minutes. Purée in a blender or food processor, and serve immediately.

MEDITERRANEAN ROASTED PUMPKIN SOUP

Serves 4

A really raunchy soup to serve before an equally powerful main course! Blend the olives into the soup if you prefer, but they do provide a color and texture contrast in the rich orange broth.

Ingredients

6 x 1-inch slices pumpkin, seeded (about 1 lb 10 oz in total)

6 large tomatoes, halved

1 large onion, sliced thick

4–5 garlic cloves

4 sprigs fresh rosemary

Salt and ground black pepper

Olive oil

2 cups water or chicken stock

½ cup pitted black olives, chopped

Shavings of fresh Parmesan cheese, to garnish

Olive oil bread, to serve

Preheat a 425°F oven. Arrange all the vegetables in a large roasting pan and tuck the garlic cloves and rosemary in amongst them. Season well, then drizzle with olive oil. Roast for 40 to 50 minutes, until starting to blacken round the edges. The pumpkin should be tender when the other vegetables are ready. Allow the vegetables to cool slightly.

Cut the flesh away from the skin of the pumpkin and chop roughly. Remove the rosemary, then scrape all the vegetables into a blender or food processor, and add the pumpkin flesh. Blend until smooth, then rub the soup through a fine strainer into a pan.

Add the water or stock, then heat the soup slowly until almost at a boil. Season well with salt and pepper, then stir in the chopped olives. Ladle into warmed bowls, garnish with a few shavings of Parmesan, then serve with plenty of olive oil bread for dunking.

GRANNY'S GARLIC AND BREAD SOUP

Serves 4

Bread and garlic soups are often eaten for supper in Spain. This one is fortified with eggs and canned tuna, which probably replaces the traditional salt cod.

Ingredients

6 garlic cloves, peeled

6 Tbsp olive oil

4 slices stale bread

4¼ cups light chicken stock

4 oz can tuna, drained and flaked

Salt

1 tsp hot paprika, or sweet paprika plus a pinch of cayenne pepper

4 eggs

½ tsp cumin seeds, well crushed

Put the garlic and oil in a casserole over medium heat. Remove and reserve the garlic the moment it looks cooked. Then fry the bread on both sides until golden. Add the stock and bring to a simmer, stirring to break up the bread. Add the garlic and flaked tuna and season with salt and paprika.

Break in the eggs and poach gently for 5 minutes. Sprinkle the cumin over the top before serving.

IRISH BARLEY SOUP

Serves 6

Leeks grew wild in Ireland for many centuries and they are still as much a part of the Irish diet as oats and barley.
Combining pearl barley with leeks in this tasty soup makes a very traditional dish.

Ingredients

10½ oz leeks, sliced fine

2 Tbsp olive oil

⅔ cup shredded spinach

¼ cup pearl barley

3¼ pt well-flavored chicken or vegetable
stock

Bouquet garni

Salt and ground black pepper

2 bay leaves

¼ cup heavy cream (optional)

Cook the leeks in the oil until softened but not browned, then add the spinach, and cook briefly until wilted. Add the barley, stock, and *bouquet garni*, then bring to a boil. Season lightly and add the bay leaves, then cover the pan, and simmer for about 1½ hours, until the barley is tender.

Remove the *bouquet garni* and bay leaves. Season to taste, then stir in the cream, if using, and serve immediately with fresh crusty bread.

YOGURT SOUP

Serves 4

This is the perfect kind of soup that you can serve to someone who is feeling a little "under the weather."

Ingredients

1 Tbsp butter or margarine
1 Tbsp flour
Generous 1 cup plain yogurt, strained
4 cups chicken stock
1 Tbsp rice, washed and drained (optional)
Salt and ground black pepper
Dried mint and paprika, to garnish
Croutons, to serve

Heat the butter or margarine in a large saucepan and add the flour. Stirring continuously, brown gently over medium heat until smooth. Mix in the yogurt, and stir thoroughly, then slowly add the chicken stock.

Bring to a boil and add the rice, if using. Season well, cover and simmer gently for about 15 minutes, or until the rice is soft. Garnish with dried mint and paprika, and serve hot with croutons.

TOMATO AND SWEET POTATO SOUP

Serves 6

Ingredients

1 Tbsp oil

1 Tbsp butter or margarine

2 onions, chopped fine

½ lb sweet potatoes, peeled and diced

3 medium tomatoes, skinned and chopped fine

2½ cups chicken stock

1 tsp salt

1 tsp chopped fresh thyme

Juice and shredded rind of 1 orange

Juice and shredded rind of 1 lemon or lime

Ground black pepper

Slices of lemon, orange, and tomato, to garnish

Heat the oil and butter or margarine in a large pan. Add the onions, and cook them slowly until they are soft.

Add the sweet potatoes, tomatoes, chicken stock, salt, thyme, orange juice and rind, lemon or lime juice and rind, and freshly ground black pepper to taste. Bring to a boil, then lower the heat, cover the pan, and simmer for about 25 minutes.

Liquidize the soup in a blender, then return it to the pan, and simmer for 5 more minutes to heat it through.

Serve it in warmed soup bowls, garnished with a slice of lemon, orange, and tomato.

PEANUT SOUP

Serves 4

Ingredients

½ stick butter or margarine
1 onion, grated
1 celery stalk, chopped
1 garlic clove, crushed
1 sprig fresh thyme, chopped
1 Tbsp flour
3¾ cups chicken stock
½ cup crunchy peanut butter or 2¼ cups coarsely ground peanuts
2 cups milk
2 tsp salt
½ tsp ground black pepper
¼ green bell pepper, seeded and chopped

Melt the butter or margarine in a large pan over low heat. Add the onion, celery, garlic, and thyme. Cook for 5 minutes, stirring all the time, then gradually add the flour and stock, still stirring constantly. Increase the heat, then stir in the peanut butter or peanuts, and cook over medium-low heat for 10 minutes.

Reduce the heat and add the milk, salt, and pepper. Simmer gently for about 15 minutes.

Serve very hot, garnished with the chopped green bell pepper.

CREME SAINT-GERMAIN

Serves 4–6

One of the classic Scandinavian soups Grön Soppa *with a mild, delicate flavor, which gets a kick from the horseradish cream.*

Ingredients

1 medium onion, sliced
2 Tbsp butter or margarine
4¼ cups veal or chicken stock
11 oz fresh shelled peas, or 1 small packet frozen peas
1 Tbsp flour
1–2 Tbsp brandy or Madeira
Salt and ground black pepper
1 egg yolk
⅓ cup light cream

For the horseradish cream

⅔ cup heavy cream
2–2½ tsp shredded horseradish

For the cheese croutons

1¾ cups flour
4 oz Swiss cheese, shredded
A pinch of salt
1 stick butter or margarine
2 Tbsp ice water
1 egg, to glaze

To make the horseradish cream, simply mix the cream and shredded horseradish together.

For the croutons, mix the flour, cheese, and salt together. Crumble the margarine or butter into the mixture. Add the water and quickly mix the pastry together into a ball. Let the pastry rest in a cool place for 30 minutes.

Meanwhile preheat a 475°F oven. Roll out the pastry to a thickness of ⅛ inch and cut out croutons. Brush with beaten egg and place on a baking sheet. Bake until golden brown, about 5 to 8 minutes.

Fry the onion in 1 tablespoon of the butter or margarine, without browning. Pour in the stock and add the peas. Boil the mixture for 15 minutes. Blend in a food processor, then strain.

Melt the rest of the butter or margarine and stir in the flour. Cook for 2 to 3 minutes, stirring. Gradually add the strained soup and stir in the brandy or wine and season to taste.

Whisk the egg yolk and cream in a soup terrine and pour in the soup, stirring vigorously. Serve the soup in warmed bowls garnished with horseradish cream and cheese croutons.

◀ *Creme Saint-Germain*

CREAMY CHESTNUT SOUP

Serves 4

Chestnuts make a delicious, creamy winter soup, delicately flavored with a little cinnamon.

Ingredients

1 lb chestnuts unshelled or 12 oz peeled
Salt and ground black pepper
1 thick slice bread
4 Tbsp olive oil
2 Tbsp red wine vinegar
About 3 cups light chicken stock
1/8 tsp ground cinnamon

Slash the chestnut shells across the fat part of the nut, drop into a large pan, and cover with cold water with a little salt. Bring to a boil and cook for 20 minutes. Let them cool (but leave under water).

Peel the chestnuts, removing the brown skin too.

Fry the bread in the oil then put it in a blender or food processor and purée with the vinegar. Reserve a handful of coarse nuts (chopped) to add texture to the soup and add the rest to the blender, a little at a time, with some of the stock. Purée to a cream.

Return the creamed soup to the pan, taste, and season with salt and pepper. Add the cinnamon and chopped nuts, heat through and serve.

PIMENTO AND PASTA SOUP

Serves 4

This delicious, wholesome, filling soup can be served with your favorite pasta shapes.

Ingredients

14 oz can pimento, drained

2¼ cups vegetable stock

Salt and ground black pepper

1 Tbsp ground coriander

8 oz cooked pasta shapes, such as tortelloni, shells, bows, etc

Fresh cilantro, to garnish

Place the pimento in a food processor or blender with a steel blade, and purée until smooth. Transfer to a large pan and add the vegetable stock, salt and pepper, and ground coriander. Stir and cook over gentle heat for about 10 minutes.

Add the cooked pasta shapes and cook for a further 2 to 3 minutes, until heated through. Serve garnished with fresh cilantro.

TOMATO-ORANGE SOUP

Serves 4

The orange in this soup brings out the sweet-acidic flavor of beefsteak tomatoes.

Ingredients

2¼ lb ripe tomatoes, blanched, peeled, and quartered (or canned whole tomatoes, undrained)

½ cup firmly packed fresh basil leaves

3 x ½-inch strip orange peel

2 Tbsp chopped scallions (white part only)

1 tsp sugar

2 Tbsp lime or lemon juice

1 cup orange juice

1 Tbsp cornstarch

2 Tbsp minced cilantro, chives, or parsley

Salt and ground black pepper

Combine the tomatoes, basil, orange peel, scallion, sugar, and lime or lemon juice in a medium pan. Cover and bring to a boil. Lower the heat immediately and simmer, covered, for 15 minutes. Remove the orange peel. Purée the mixture in a blender or food processor and strain through a strainer if desired to discard any seeds. Return the liquid to the pan.

Stir together the orange juice and cornstarch in a small bowl until smooth. Stir into the tomato mixture. Cook over medium heat, stirring constantly, until the mixture thickens and comes to a boil. Lower the heat, stir in the cilantro, chives, or parsley, and salt and pepper to taste. Garnish with croutons, if desired.

SWEET POTATO AND LEEK SOUP

Serves 6

If you are able to find sweet potatoes with yellow flesh and a consistency more like potatoes than yams, omit the white potato from this recipe.

Ingredients

1 Tbsp butter

4 medium leeks, sliced thin

1¾ lb sweet potatoes, peeled and cubed

1 medium white potato, cubed

4 cups water

Salt and ground black pepper

Grated fresh nutmeg

2½ cups chicken stock

⅔ cup heavy cream

3 Tbsp snipped fresh chives

Melt the butter in a large, heavy pan over medium-low heat. Add the leeks, cover, and cook for 6 to 8 minutes, or until softened.

Add the sweet potatoes, white potato, and water. Season with salt, black pepper, and nutmeg. Bring to a boil over high heat. Reduce the heat and simmer, partially covered, for 20 minutes until the vegetables are very tender, stirring occasionally.

Transfer the vegetables and cooking liquid to a blender or a food processor fitted with a steel blade and purée until smooth, working in batches if necessary. Strain the mixture back into the saucepan, pressing firmly with the back of a spoon to extract as much liquid as possible. Stir in the stock, set over low heat, and simmer for 10 to 15 minutes, or until heated through. Taste and adjust the seasoning.

Using an electric mixer or whisk, whip the cream with a pinch of salt until soft peaks form. Stir in the chives.

Ladle the soup into warm bowls or soup plates and garnish with the chive-flavored whipped cream.

Tomato-Orange Soup ▶

CLEAR CEP SOUP

Serves 4

This is a formal soup for special occasions. It has a strong mushroom flavor with the delicate addition of vegetables and pasta to create the contrasting textures.

Ingredients

1 oz dried ceps

2½ cups warm water

1 leek

1 carrot

3 oz conchigliette piccole (tiny pasta shells), cooked

Salt and ground black pepper

Italian parsley, to garnish

Place the ceps in the warm water, and leave to soak for about 30 minutes. Drain the ceps, reserving the liquid in a pan.

Slice the ceps, and shred the leek and carrot. Add the vegetables to the mushroom stock and cook over medium heat for about 10 minutes, until the vegetables are tender.

Add the cooked pasta shells, and season with salt and ground black pepper. Cook for a further minute. Serve garnished with the parsley leaves.

ROASTED ACORN SQUASH SOUP WITH CUCUMBER SALSA

Serves 4

This creamy, nutty flavored soup is further enhanced by a subtly spicy cucumber salsa.

Ingredients

1 acorn squash (weighing about 1 lb 4 oz) quartered
Salt and freshly grated nutmeg
Olive oil
1 large onion, chopped fine
2 slices Canadian bacon, rinded and chopped
2 large carrots, sliced
4–5 young lovage leaves, shredded fine, or 3 bay leaves
4 cups well-flavored vegetable stock
Ground black pepper
1 cup milk

For the salsa

1 Tbsp coriander seeds
½ medium cucumber, seeded and diced
1 mild green chile, seeded and chopped fine
1 small red onion, chopped fine
1 fresh tomato, seeded and chopped
1 garlic clove, chopped fine
1-inch piece fresh ginger root, shredded

Cook's tip

Roasting hard-skinned squashes before final cooking makes them easier to cut and prepare, and brings out their nutty flavor.

Preheat a 425°F oven. Scrape the seeds out of the squash, then arrange the pieces in a roasting pan, and season lightly with salt and nutmeg. Drizzle with a little olive oil, then roast the squash for 45 minutes, or until tender. Leave to cool.

Meanwhile, cook the onion, bacon, and carrots with 1 tablespoon of olive oil in a covered pan for 4 to 5 minutes, until the vegetables are tender. Scoop the roasted squash from the skin, chop it roughly, then add it to the pan with the lovage or bay, and stock. Season lightly with salt and pepper, then bring to a boil. Cover the pan and simmer gently for 30 minutes.

Meanwhile, prepare the salsa. Heat a small frying pan over medium heat until hot, then add the coriander seeds and fry for 1 minute, until roasted and fragrant. Crush the seeds lightly using a pestle and mortar, or use the end of a rolling pin. Add all the other salsa ingredients except the ginger. Finally, gather up the ginger shreds in your hands and squeeze just the juice into the mixture. Leave to stand for 30 minutes, to allow the flavors to blend.

Cool the soup slightly, then blend until smooth in a blender or food processor, adding the milk. Season to taste and reheat if necessary. Serve the soup with a spoonful of salsa in each portion.

COLD VEGETABLE SOUPS

CHILLED GREEN PEA SOUP

Serves 6

This soup is a stunning bright green color. It is simple to make and quite tasty using frozen peas, but if you are able to find fresh-picked young garden peas, you are in for a real gourmet treat.

Ingredients

1 Tbsp butter
4 shallots, chopped fine
6 cups shelled fresh peas or thawed frozen peas
4 cups water
Salt and ground black pepper
⅔ cup heavy cream
2 Tbsp chopped fresh mint
12–18 small snow peas, blanched and chilled, to garnish

Melt the butter in a large pan over medium-low heat. Add the shallots and cook, stirring occasionally, until they begin to soften, about 5 minutes.

Add the peas and water. Season with salt and a little pepper. Simmer, covered, stirring occasionally, until the vegetables are tender, about 12 minutes for frozen or young fresh peas, or up to 18 minutes for large peas.

Transfer the solids to a blender or a food processor fitted with a steel blade. Add some of the cooking liquid and purée until smooth, working in batches if necessary. Strain into a bowl with the remaining cooking liquid, allow to stand until cool, cover, and chill until cold.

Using an electric mixer or whisk, whip the cream in a chilled bowl until soft peaks form. Stir in the mint.

Thin the soup with a little cold water, if needed, and adjust the seasoning. Ladle into chilled soup plates and garnish each with a dollop of cream and 2 or 3 snow peas.

Cook's tip
You will need 5–6 lb
of fresh peas in the pod to
obtain 6 cups of shelled peas.

CHILLED VEGETABLE SOUP

Serves 4–6

This is an extraordinarily refreshing soup—like a liquid salad. Based on ingredients found all over the Central Republics of Russia, it is a refined variation on a common theme.

Ingredients

3 garlic cloves
4 thick slices Greek or baguette, crusts removed
½ stick butter
2 red onions, sliced thin
8 radishes, sliced thin
7 large ripe tomatoes, skinned, seeded, and chopped
½ cucumber, peeled and sliced thin
Salt and ground black pepper
A large dash of Tabasco
5 Tbsp vegetable oil
1 Tbsp lemon juice
14-oz can chicken consommé
⅔ cup Greek-style yogurt
8 scallions, chopped fine

Finely chop two of the garlic cloves and set aside. Halve and use the remaining clove to rub over the bread slices. Roughly cut them into croutons.

Heat the butter in a frying pan and sauté the croutons until golden. Drain and set aside.

In a large bowl, combine the chopped garlic, red onions, radishes, tomatoes, cucumber, seasoning to taste, and the Tabasco. In a small bowl, whisk together the oil and lemon juice, then pour over the salad and chill for about 1 hour.

Place the chicken consommé in the refrigerator 30 minutes before you make the soup. Just before serving, add the chilled consommé to the bowl and stir it in thoroughly, then stir in the yogurt. Sprinkle with the scallions, and serve the croutons in a separate bowl.

COLD BORSCHT

Serves 6

There is no single definitive recipe for Borscht, the popular Eastern European peasant soup. In fact, there seem to be almost limitless variations—some with meat, some with beans, some mainly cabbage, others mainly beets. This meatless version offers a balanced combination of vegetable flavors that meld when chilled.

Ingredients

½ medium red cabbage, cored and chopped coarse

1 Tbsp vegetable oil

1 large onion, chopped

1 large leek, split and sliced

1 large carrot, sliced thin

1 medium parsnip, sliced thin

⅔ cup red wine

5 cups chicken stock or water, plus more if needed

6 medium beets, peeled and cubed

4 tomatoes, peeled, seeded, and chopped coarse

Bay leaf

1 tsp sherry vinegar or red wine vinegar

Sour cream or yogurt

Chopped fresh dill, to garnish

Cover the cabbage with cold water. Set over high heat, bring to a boil, and boil for 3 minutes. Drain.

Heat the oil in a large pan over medium-low heat and add the onion and leek. Cover and sweat the vegetables until soft, about 5 minutes, stirring occasionally. Add the carrot, parsnip, blanched cabbage, and wine. Bring to a boil and add the stock or water, beets, tomatoes, and bay leaf. Bring back to a boil, reduce the heat, and simmer until all the vegetables are just tender, about 1¼ hours.

Remove the bay leaf and, using a slotted spoon, transfer the solids to a blender or food processor fitted with a steel blade, working in batches if necessary. Add some of the cooking liquid and purée until smooth.

Strain the purée and any remaining cooking liquid into a large bowl. Stir in the vinegar, leave to cool, and chill until cold. If you wish, thin the soup with water or more stock.

Season to taste with salt and pepper, and add a little more vinegar, if liked. Ladle into chilled soup bowls or plates, top each with a dollop of sour cream or yogurt and sprinkle with dill.

COLD AVOCADO SOUP

Serves 4–6

Ingredients

1 or 2 green Anaheim chiles
1 Tbsp oil
3 large ripe avocados
²⁄₃ cup chicken or vegetable stock
1¼ cups light cream
²⁄₃ cup milk
1 to 2 Tbsp lime juice
Salt and white pepper
Snipped fresh chives and sour cream, to garnish

Preheat the broiler to high. Cut the chiles in half and discard the seeds. Place in a broiler pan, skin-side uppermost, and drizzle with the oil. Broil for 5 minutes, or until the skin has blistered. Remove from the heat and leave to cool.

Discard the skin and membrane from the chiles and roughly chop. Put into a food processor. Peel and seed the avocados, then roughly chop, and put into the processor with the stock. Blend to form a smooth purée.

With the machine still running at low speed, add the cream, then add the milk slowly.

Stir in the lime juice and seasoning to taste. Pour into a soup tureen and chill for at least 1 hour. Serve garnished with snipped fresh chives and sour cream.

HUNGARIAN CHERRY PEPPER SOUP

Serves 4

Ingredients

2 Hungarian cherry peppers (or red bell peppers)

2 Tbsp sunflower oil

1 onion, chopped fine

1 garlic clove, minced

2½ cups vegetable or chicken stock

8 oz ripe tomatoes, peeled and seeded

Salt and ground black pepper

2 Tbsp light cream, and chopped Hungarian cherry pepper, to serve

Preheat the broiler. Rinse the bell peppers and cut in half, discarding the seeds. Place, skin-side up, on a sheet of aluminum foil in a broiler pan under the broiler. Drizzle with 1 tablespoon of the oil and broil for 5 to 10 minutes, or until the skins have blistered. Remove from the heat and leave to cool. When cool, remove the skins and roughly chop.

Meanwhile, heat the remaining oil in a pan and sauté the onion and garlic for 5 minutes, or until transparent but not browned. Add the chopped peppers and then the stock. Roughly chop the tomatoes and add to the pan with seasoning to taste. Bring to a boil, then cover, and simmer gently for 15 minutes, or until the peppers are soft.

Leave to cool, then purée in a food processor or strainer. Chill for 1 hour.

To serve, add the cream and swirl lightly, then sprinkle with a little chopped cherry pepper.

ICED ALMOND AND GARLIC SOUP

Serves 4

This Spanish recipe dates from the tenth century. It is one of numerous versions of gazpacho popular all over Spain.

Ingredients

3 cups soft white bread crumbs, made from flavorful homemade-style bread

1½ cups blanched almonds, lightly toasted

2 garlic cloves, minced

A pinch of salt

2 tsp sherry vinegar

6 Tbsp extra virgin olive oil

3 cups water

1 cup seedless white grapes, to garnish

Soak the bread crumbs in cold water to cover for 5 minutes.

Put the almonds, garlic, and salt in a food processor fitted with a steel blade and process until the nuts are finely ground. Strain the bread crumbs, pressing with the back of a spoon to extract more water. Add to the almond mixture and process until pasty.

Add the vinegar and, with the machine running, pour the oil through the feed tube, then slowly pour in the water, stopping to scrape down the sides several times. Strain into a bowl and chill until very cold.

Ladle over ice cubes into a chilled tureen or soup plates and garnish with the grapes, cut in half.

Hungarian Cherry Pepper Soup ▶

ZUCCHINI AND MINT SOUP

Serves 4

This delicate soup has a silky texture and a hint of mint.

Ingredients

3½ cups vegetable stock
1 onion, chopped
1 garlic clove, minced
3 zucchini, shredded
1 large potato, scrubbed and chopped
1 Tbsp chopped fresh mint
Ground black pepper
⅔ cup low-fat plain yogurt
Mint sprigs and zucchini strips, to garnish

Put half of the vegetable stock in a large pan, add the onion and garlic, and cook for 5 minutes over a gentle heat until the onion softens. Add the shredded zucchini, potato, and the remaining stock. Stir in the mint and cook over gentle heat for 20 minutes or until the potato is cooked.

Transfer the soup to a food processor and blend for 10 seconds, until almost smooth. Turn the soup into a bowl, season, and stir in the yogurt. Cover and chill for 2 hours. Spoon the soup into individual serving bowls or a soup tureen, garnish, and serve.

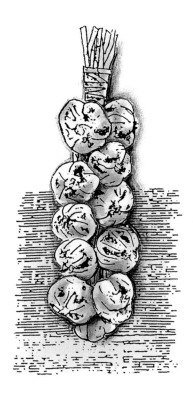

CUCUMBER COOLER

Serves 6

This soup is so refreshing—cool as the proverbial cucumber with a subtle hint of mint.

Ingredients

2 large cucumbers
1¼ cups plain yogurt (preferably Greek-style)
¾ cup buttermilk
1–2 garlic cloves, very finely minced
2 Tbsp chopped fine fresh mint
Salt and ground black pepper
Fresh lemon juice
Mint leaves, to garnish

Cut 12 thin slices from one of the cucumbers and reserve, covered, for garnishing. Peel the cucumbers, halve lengthwise, and scoop out the seeds with the tip of a small spoon.

Shred the cucumbers and transfer to a large bowl. Stir in the yogurt, buttermilk, garlic, and mint. Season to taste with salt and pepper and a few drops of lemon juice.

Chill until cold, at least 1 hour. Ladle into chilled soup plates and garnish with the reserved cucumber slices and mint leaves.

Zucchini and Mint Soup ▶

CHILLED CUCUMBER AND GREEN CHILE SOUP

Serves 6

This soup is highly spiced which counteracts the "flavor numbing" effect of chilling.

Ingredients

4 large scallions, trimmed and sliced
1 lemon grass stalk, bruised and chopped fine
1–2 garlic cloves, crushed
2 each green and caribe chiles, seeded and chopped fine, or 3 green chiles
2 lime leaves, shredded fine
1 vegetable stock cube, crumbled
4 cups water
1 large cucumber, weighing about 1 lb, seeded and chopped
1 cup plain yogurt
1 Tbsp fish sauce
Salt
2 Tbsp chopped fresh cilantro

Place the scallions, lemon grass, garlic, chiles, and lime leaves in a pan with the stock cube. Pour in the water, then bring to a boil. Add the cucumber, cover the pan, remove from heat, and leave to marinate for 1 hour.

Purée the soup in a blender or food processor until smooth, then press the mixture through a fine strainer with the back of a ladle. Whisk in the yogurt and fish sauce, then season the soup to taste with a little salt if necessary. Chill very well, for at least 2 hours.

Add the cilantro to the soup just before serving, and spoon the soup over about a tablespoon of crushed ice in each individual bowl.

WHITE GAZPACHO

Serves 4–6

Chop the vegetables by hand for gazpacho to achieve a thick, not puréed soup. While it takes a little longer to do it this way, another benefit is that you can serve the vegetables separately from the soup and let your family or guests spoon in the items they want. Tortilla chips make wonderful "crackers" for serving with gazpacho.

Ingredients

3 seedless cucumbers, peeled and chopped
3 cloves garlic, minced
3 cups chicken stock
2 Tbsp mild vinegar or lime juice
1½ cups buttermilk
3–4 Tbsp chopped scallions
¼ cup chopped fresh dill
Chive flowers, to garnish (optional)

In a large bowl, combine the cucumbers, garlic, stock, vinegar or lime juice, buttermilk, scallions, and dill. Cover and chill overnight to allow the flavors to mellow.

Stir the soup thoroughly and garnish with chive flowers before serving, if using.

◄ *Chilled Cucumber and Green Chile Soup*

ICY RED GAZPACHO SOUP

Serves 6

This icy, vinegared soup is made creamy with bread and oil. Serve garnished with lots of extras from little bowls.

Ingredients

2 slices stale white bread, crusts removed

1 small onion, chopped

2 garlic cloves, chopped fine

2 Tbsp olive oil

1 tsp coarse salt

1 cucumber, seeded and chopped, with some skin removed

1 large red bell pepper, seeded and chopped rough

4–5 big ripe red tomatoes, skinned and seeded

2 Tbsp red wine or sherry vinegar

3½ cups ice water

A pinch of cayenne pepper

To garnish choose from

4 Tbsp fried croutons

2 hard-cooked eggs, peeled and chopped

4 Tbsp chopped bell pepper (red, green or both)

4 Tbsp chopped Spanish onion or scallions

Green or black olives, pitted and chopped

Soak the bread in water, then squeeze out. Put it in a blender or food processor with the onion, garlic, olive oil, and salt and purée.

Add the cucumber to the blender or food processor with the bell pepper, then the tomatoes and vinegar (you may have to do this in two batches in a small machine). Chill for at least 12 hours, preferably overnight, or freeze for about 30 minutes.

To serve, dilute with ice water (no ice cubes) and season to taste with the cayenne pepper. Arrange the garnishes in little dishes and pass them around on a tray for everyone to help themselves.

TOMATO AND CILANTRO SOUP

Serves 6

This summer soup makes the most of a glut of plump, juicy tomatoes. The piquant flavor of cilantro offsets them wonderfully. This would make an ideal appetizer to be served before a fish or poultry main dish.

Ingredients

3 lb ripe, plump tomatoes, roughly chopped
¾ cup tomato juice
3 Tbsp freshly squeezed orange juice
1 Greek or Italian pickled pepper, seeded
¾ tsp superfine sugar
Ice water
4 Tbsp fresh cilantro, chopped fine
¼ pt Greek-style yogurt

In a blender or food processor fitted with a metal blade, purée the tomatoes, tomato and orange juices, pepper, and sugar until as smooth as possible. Press the purée through a strainer, rubbing with a wooden spoon to force as much through as possible.

Discard the residue, and add enough ice water to thin the purée to a soup-like consistency. Stir in the cilantro, cover, and chill until cold. Pass around the yogurt separately at the table, to allow guests to add as much of it as they wish.

PULSE AND BEAN SOUPS

LENTIL SOUP

Serve 6–8

Lentils have, for many years, provided a simple, adaptable, accessible, and portable source of protein and calories. This version has a middle-Eastern flavor.

Ingredients

³⁄₄ cup green lentils	3 celery stalks, chopped
2 Tbsp olive oil	2 potatoes, diced
1 red onion, chopped fine	Salt and ground black pepper
2 garlic cloves, chopped	1 bunch of cilantro, chopped coarse
12 oz shin of veal, chopped	Lemon juice
¹⁄₂ tsp each ground cumin and cinnamon	
¹⁄₄ tsp cayenne pepper	
Generous 3 pt water	
3 small-to-medium carrots, diced	

Boil the lentils in a pan of water for at least 10 minutes, drain, and set aside. Heat the oil in a pan, then cook the onion, garlic, and veal, stirring frequently, until the onion is soft. Stir in the spices until fragrant, then add the lentils and water. Bring to a boil and skim the scum from the surface. Partly cover and simmer for about 1 hour until the meat is tender.

Add the vegetables and cook for a further 30 to 40 minutes. Season and stir in the cilantro and lemon juice to taste. Serve straight away.

GARBANZO SOUP

Serves 4

This soup is usually extremely rich. The taste of all the garlic mellows with the long cooking. Add some ground spices, such as cumin, coriander, and paprika if you like.

Ingredients

6 Tbsp olive oil
10 garlic cloves, crushed
12 oz garbanzo beans, soaked overnight and drained
5 pt water
1 red onion, chopped fine
2 carrots, chopped
1 head of celery, chopped
Salt and ground black pepper
Lemon juice
1 bunch of cilantro, chopped

Heat 4 tablespoons oil in a large pan, then cook the garlic until fragrant. Stir in the garbanzos, then add the water, and bring to a boil. Skim the scum from the surface, then simmer until the garbanzos are tender.

Meanwhile, heat the remaining oil in a flameproof earthenware casserole, add the onion, carrots, and celery, cover, and cook gently for about 20 minutes.

Add the vegetables to the garbanzos, then purée half the mixture in a food processor or blender, or rub through a strainer. Stir back into the soup and reheat. Add seasoning and lemon juice to taste, and sprinkle with cilantro. Serve immediately with warm fresh bread.

◀ *Lentil Soup*

LEBANESE COUSCOUS SOUP

Serves 6

Couscous, tiny grains made from semolina, is usually steamed over a stew or stock. In this recipe, the couscous is used to thicken a richly spiced onion soup.

Ingredients

4 large onions, sliced fine
3 garlic cloves, sliced fine
2 Tbsp vegetable oil
1 Tbsp butter
1 red chile, seeded and chopped fine
1 tsp mild chili powder
½ tsp ground turmeric
1 tsp ground coriander
Salt and ground black pepper
4¼ pt vegetable or chicken stock
¼ cup couscous
Chopped fresh cilantro, to garnish

Cook the onions and garlic in the oil and melted butter until well browned. This will take about 15 minutes over medium high heat. You must let the onions brown to achieve a rich color for the finished soup.

Stir in the chopped chile and the spices and cook over low heat for a further 1 to 2 minutes before adding the stock. Season lightly then bring to a boil. Cover and simmer gently for 30 minutes.

Stir the couscous into the soup, return to a boil, and simmer for a further 10 minutes. Season to taste, then garnish with the cilantro and serve immediately.

ARMENIAN SOUP

Serves 6

A spicy lentil soup, sweetened and thickened with apricots and golden raisins. Ginger, cumin, and cinnamon make an exotic trio of seasonings.

Ingredients

1 large onion, chopped fine
2 Tbsp olive oil
1 tsp ground ginger
1 tsp ground cumin
½ tsp ground cinnamon
2 tomatoes, diced
¾ cup red lentils
3¼ pt well-flavored vegetable stock
Salt and ground black pepper

3½ oz ready-to-eat dried apricots, chopped rough
⅓ cup golden raisins
Sour cream (optional)

Cook the onion in the oil in a large pan until soft, then add the spices, and cook for 1 minute over low heat. Add the tomatoes and lentils, then stir in the stock, and bring the soup slowly to a boil. Season well, add the dried fruits, then cover, and simmer for 30 minutes, until the lentils and vegetables are soft.

Season the soup to taste. It may be puréed if preferred, then thinned down with a little extra stock or water. Serve with a dollop of sour cream.

Lebanese Couscous Soup ▶

GALICIAN BEAN, PORK, AND GREENS SOUP

Serves 6

This is a traditional springtime soup from Galicia in Spain. The flavor comes from salt meat: use fresh spareribs or salt pork, whichever is easiest.

Ingredients

³/₄ lb pork spareribs or 4 oz salt pork

Salt

1 lb smoked ham knuckle bone with meat

1¼ cups dried navy beans, soaked overnight

1 lb new potatoes

Ground black pepper

7 oz tender turnip leaves or kale

If using pork spareribs, rub them well with salt. Alternatively, salt pork must be blanched. Put it with the ham knuckle bone in a pan, cover with cold water, and bring to a boil. Simmer for 5 minutes then drain. Cube the pork.

Drain the beans and put them, with the meat and bones, into a casserole. Add 4¼ pints water, bring to a simmer, skim off any scum, then cook gently, covered, for 1 hour.

Add the potatoes and simmer until done (about 20 minutes). Remove all the bones from the pot and taste the stock. Season with salt and pepper as necessary. Add the greens and simmer for 5 to 10 minutes. Return all the meat from the bones to the pan. To thicken the liquid a little, mash in a few potatoes.

ASTURIAN BEAN AND SAUSAGE POT

Serves 6

Fabada Asturiana, *is one of the world's most famous bean pots. It is flavored with cured sausages, to give an incredible richness to the flat, white lima beans.*

Ingredients

1 lb 10 oz dried lima beans
1½ lb salt pork
1½ lb smoked ham knuckle or back, skin slashed
6 black peppercorns, crushed
1 tsp paprika
A pinch of powdered saffron
1 bay leaf
2 Tbsp oil (optional)
4 garlic cloves, chopped
1 lb chorizos or smoked sausages, like kabanos
6 oz morcilla or blood sausage

Choose a stockpot that holds at least 12½ pints. Cover the beans, in a bowl, with plenty of boiling water. Put the salt meat (salt pork and ham bone) into the pot and cover with cold water. Bring to a boil, then drain the meat, and return to the stockpot.

Drain the beans then add to the pot with the peppercorns, paprika, saffron, and bay leaf. Add 4¾ pints water. Bring slowly to a boil, then simmer very gently on minimum heat for 2 hours. A big pot on a small burner is best, and better still with a heat diffuser. Check occasionally that the beans are still covered, but do not stir (or they will break up).

Remove the ham bone and salt pork, to cool a little. Strip off the skin and fat, and take about 2 tablespoons of chopped fat for frying (or use oil). Sweat this in a shallow skillet. In the fat it makes, fry the garlic lightly, then spoon it into the beans.

Fry the sliced sausages and morcilla or blood sausage (discarding any artificial casings). Stir into the pot with the pan fat.

Remove all the meat from the ham bone. Chop it, and the salt pork or beef, and return to the pot; simmer over a medium heat for a few minutes. Check the seasonings (there should be enough salt from the meat). Serve with fresh greens.

MEXICAN BEAN SOUP

Serves 6

Pinto beans are traditionally used in this soup; if you are unable to get them, use only kidney beans to make this thick and spicy soup.

Ingredients

²/₃ cup red kidney beans, soaked overnight

²/₃ cup pinto beans, soaked overnight

1 large onion, chopped fine

1 Tbsp oil

1 red chile, seeded and chopped fine

1 large garlic clove, sliced fine

1 tsp mild chili powder

1 Tbsp cilantro leaves

3¼ pt well-flavored vegetable stock

1 Tbsp tomato paste

Salt and ground black pepper

½ cup Cheddar cheese, shredded

Guacamole, to serve

Drain the beans and rinse them thoroughly under cold running water, then set aside until needed. Cook the onion in the oil until soft, then add the chile, garlic, and chili powder, and cook for another minute.

Stir the beans into the pan then add the cilantro, stock, tomato paste, and seasonings. Bring the soup to a boil and boil for 10 minutes, then simmer slowly for 45 to 60 minutes, until the beans are soft. Allow the soup to cool, then purée until smooth in a blender or food processor. Rinse the pan then return the soup to it and reheat gently, seasoning with salt and pepper.

Scatter the cheese over the soup just before serving and set out a dish of guacamole (see below).

GUACAMOLE

Serves 4

Ingredients

2 ripe avocados

1½ cups peeled, seeded, and chopped fine ripe tomatoes

1 bunch scallions, trimmed and chopped

2 serrano chiles, seeded and chopped fine

1 or 2 jalapeño chiles, seeded and chopped fine

2 Tbsp lime juice

1½ Tbsp chopped fresh cilantro

Salt and ground black pepper

Shredded lime rind, to garnish

Peel the avocados and discard the seeds. Mash the flesh with a potato masher or fork.

Add the chopped tomato and scallions with the chiles and mix together well. Stir in the lime juice with the cilantro and seasoning to taste. Turn into a serving bowl and fork the top.

Sprinkle with the lime rind just before serving with the soup. It should be eaten immediately but if it has to be kept, put one of the avocado seeds in the middle, cover and chill for no longer than 1 hour.

PASTA BEAN SOUP

Serves 4–6

A nutritious meal in itself—low-fat and full of protein. Serve with warm, crusty garlic bread.

Ingredients

2 Tbsp olive oil

3 garlic cloves, minced

4 Tbsp chopped fresh parsley

5 oz dried whole-wheat gnocchi piccoli (shells)

3 pt vegetable stock

3 Tbsp vegetable or tomato paste

14 oz can mixed beans, such as borlotti, kidney, cannellini, etc, drained

Salt and ground black pepper

Freshly shredded Parmesan cheese, to serve

Heat the olive oil in a large pan, and sauté the garlic with the chopped parsley for about 2 minutes. Add the gnocchi piccoli and cook for 1 to 2 minutes, stirring constantly.

Pour in the vegetable stock, and add the vegetable or tomato paste. Bring to a boil, reduce the heat, then simmer for about 10 minutes, stirring occasionally, until the pasta is tender.

Add the beans, and season with salt and freshly ground black pepper. Continue to cook for a further 5 minutes, then serve with a little freshly shredded Parmesan cheese.

GARBANZO WITH SPINACH

Serves 6

This soup-stew is made with, or without, salt cod. The latter makes a pleasant vegetarian dish.

Ingredients

7 oz salt cod, soaked overnight (optional)
1²⁄₃ cup garbanzo beans, soaked overnight
2 onions, 1 whole, peeled, 1 chopped
1 clove
1 large carrot
1 bay leaf
2–3 parsley stalks, bruised
3 Tbsp olive oil
2 garlic cloves, chopped fine
2 ripe tomatoes, skinned and chopped
1 tsp paprika
Salt and ground black pepper
1³⁄₄ lb spinach, trimmed and washed
2 hard-cooked eggs, peeled and chopped

Remove the bones and skin from the salt cod (if using) and shred the flesh. Put the drained garbanzos, salt cod, 1 whole onion stuck with a clove, whole carrot, bay leaf, and parsley stalks into a large casserole and add 5 cups water. Bring slowly to a simmer, skim off the bubbles, then cover and simmer for 1½ to 2 hours.

Heat the oil in a shallow frying pan and fry the chopped onion. As it softens add the garlic, tomatoes, and paprika. Cook down to a sauce, seasoning with salt and pepper,

Add the spinach to a panful of boiling water—just in and out for young spinach, but cook older leaves for 2 to 3 minutes. Drain and chop.

When the garbanzos are almost tender, remove the bay leaf, parsley stalks, whole onion, and carrot. Discard the clove and purée the onion and carrot in a blender or food processor with 3 tablespoons of the garbanzos and half a ladleful of their liquid. Check the amount of liquid: the garbanzos should be barely covered at this point. Pour off some water if necessary.

Add the tomato sauce and onion purée to the casserole. Taste for seasoning—plenty is needed. Add the spinach, simmer for another 20 minutes or so to blend the flavors, then check that the garbanzos are tender. Traditionally the soup is served with chopped hard-cooked egg on top.

BEAN SOUP

Serves 4–6

Ingredients

1 cup navy beans
1–2 Tbsp oil
1 onion, chopped
1 garlic clove, chopped
2 carrots, chopped
2 celery stalks, sliced
7 oz tomatoes, peeled (or a small can)
1 slice lemon
Soy sauce
Salt and ground black pepper
Chopped fresh parsley

Soak the beans overnight. Bring to a boil in a large pan of water (about 5 cups) and simmer until tender.

Meanwhile, heat the oil in a frying pan and cook the onion and garlic until soft. Add the carrots, celery, and tomatoes, in that order, stirring all the while.

Tip the vegetables into the pan with the cooked beans. Add the slice of lemon and soy sauce. Taste and adjust the seasoning. Heat through and serve sprinkled with chopped parsley. The soup may be partly blended if you like.

Chickpeas with Spinach ▶

TUSCAN WHITE BEAN AND KALE SOUP

Serves 6

This soup is perfect for a fireside supper on a winter's evening. Serve it with warm focaccio or garlic bread.

Ingredients

1¼ cups dried borlotti or navy beans, soaked overnight

1 Tbsp olive oil

3½ oz pancetta or smoked lean bacon, chopped

1 onion, chopped fine

1 shallot, chopped fine

1 carrot, chopped fine

1–2 garlic cloves, minced

4 tomatoes, peeled, seeded, and chopped, or 1¾ cups canned chopped tomatoes

5 cups water

Bouquet garni (thyme and marjoram sprigs, parsley, and bay leaf)

4 oz curly kale leaves, finely chopped (2 lightly packed cups)

Freshly shredded or shaved Parmesan cheese, to serve (optional)

Salt and ground black pepper

Drain the beans, put into a pan with cold water to cover, and set over high heat. Bring to a boil and boil for 10 minutes. Drain and add fresh cold water to cover. Bring to a boil again, drain, and rinse well.

Heat the oil in a large heavy pan over medium-high heat and add the pancetta or bacon. Cook until lightly browned, stirring frequently. Remove with a slotted spoon to drain on paper towels and pour off all but 1 tablespoon of the fat. Reduce the heat to low, add the onion, shallot, carrot, and garlic, and cook for 3 to 4 minutes until slightly softened. Add the beans, tomatoes, water, *bouquet garni*, and pancetta or bacon, and simmer until the beans are tender, 1 to 2 hours. Season to taste with salt and pepper.

Stir in the kale and continue cooking for 15 to 20 minutes, or until it is tender. Adjust the seasoning and ladle the soup into warm bowls. Serve sprinkled with Parmesan cheese, if you like.

CABBAGE, BEAN, AND HAM SOUP

Serves 6

Serve this hearty winter soup with cornmeal bread and cheese.

Ingredients

1 cup dried lima beans
1 Tbsp olive oil
1 cup chopped onion
3 garlic cloves, minced
2 carrots, peeled and chopped
3 pt chicken stock
2 cups water
2 cups diced ham
2 sprigs of parsley
2 bay leaves
1 tsp fresh thyme or ¼ tsp dried
¼ tsp dried sage
3 cups shredded green cabbage
Salt and ground black pepper

Put the lima beans in a large pan. Add 1 quart of water. Bring the water to a boil, boil for 2 minutes. Remove the pan from the heat, and let the beans soak for 1 hour in the hot water. Drain the beans.

In a small frying pan, sauté the onion, garlic, and carrots in olive oil for 5 minutes. Put the beans and the vegetables in the large pan with the chicken stock, 2 cups water, ham, parsley, bay leaves, thyme, and sage. Simmer, uncovered, until the beans are tender, about 1 hour. Add the cabbage. Cook until the cabbage is tender, 5 minutes. Add salt and pepper to taste.

SPICY BLACK BEAN SOUP

Serves 4–6

This soup has its roots in Cuba, but it has been adapted to suit more contemporary taste.

Ingredients

2½ cups black beans

1 Tbsp olive oil

2 red onions, chopped fine

4 garlic cloves, minced

5 Tbsp brandy

4 pts water

Bouquet garni (bay leaf, thyme, and marjoram sprigs, cilantro and parsley stems, and 2–3 strips orange zest)

½ tsp cumin seeds

¼ tsp dried oregano

3–4 roasted ancho chile peppers, seeded and chopped, or ¾ tsp crushed dried chiles

1 Tbsp tomato paste

3 tomatoes, peeled, seeded, and chopped

Salt and ground black pepper

6 Tbsp sour cream

3–4 scallions, chopped fine

Cilantro leaves, to garnish

Pick over the beans to remove any small stones. Cover with cold water and leave to soak for at least 6 hours or overnight.

Drain the beans, put into a pan with cold water to cover, and set over high heat. Bring to a boil and boil for 10 minutes. Drain and rinse well.

Heat the oil in a large, heavy pan over medium-high heat, add the onions, and cook until they are just softened, 3 to 4 minutes, stirring frequently. Add the garlic and continue cooking for 2 minutes. Add the brandy, water, *bouquet garni*, cumin seeds, oregano, and chiles. When the mixture begins to bubble, stir in the tomato paste, reduce the heat to low, and simmer gently, partially covered, for 1½ to 2½ hours until the beans are tender, stirring occasionally. Remove and discard the *bouquet garni* and season with salt and pepper.

Ladle the soup into a warm tureen or bowls and top with a dollop of sour cream. Sprinkle with the scallions and garnish with cilantro.

STONE SOUP

Serves 6

The red kidney beans resemble stones in this Portuguese soup—at least, that is the theory, hence the name.

Ingredients

1 cup red kidney beans, soaked overnight and drained
4 oz piece smoked bacon
4 oz piece chorizo
1 Spanish onion, chopped
1 garlic clove, crushed
1 bay leaf
2 carrots, diced
3 celery stalks, diced
1 lb potatoes, diced
1 cup Savoy or other cabbage, shredded
4¼ cups chicken or vegetable stock
Salt and ground black pepper
¾ cup chopped fresh cilantro

Put the beans into a pan, add enough water to cover generously, and boil for 10 minutes. Cover and simmer for about 35 minutes or until the beans are almost tender. Drain and set aside.

Put the bacon into the pan and cook, turning occasionally, until much of the fat has been rendered. Stir in the chorizo, onion, and garlic, and cook, stirring occasionally, until the onion is softened.

Add the beans, bay leaf, vegetables, stock, seasoning, and most of the cilantro. Cover and simmer for about 30 minutes.

Remove the bacon and sausage from the soup. Dice the bacon and slice the sausage. Return to the soup and reheat. Sprinkle with the remaining cilantro and serve with warm crusty bread.

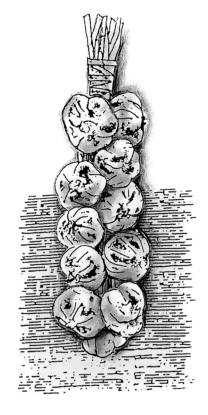

WHITE BEAN AND YUCA VICHYSSOISE

Serves 4–6

Toss some leftover bits of chorizo, ham or flank steak into this soup after it's puréed and you have a delicious and slightly different version of vichyssoise.

Ingredients

2 Tbsp plus 2 tsp olive oil, divided
4 tsp white wine
4 garlic cloves, crushed
2 Tbsp butter or margarine
2 leeks, sliced and rinsed
2 celery stalks, sliced
18-oz cans cannellini (white kidney) beans, drained and rinsed
1 lb yuca or potatoes, peeled and cut into 2-inch sections
2 × 14½-oz cans chicken stock or use stock cubes
2 tsp chopped fresh rosemary
2 tsp chopped fresh thyme leaves
2 tsp chopped fresh sage
2 bay leaves
Salt and ground white pepper
2 Tbsp snipped fresh chives, to garnish (optional)

In a small pan, heat 2 teaspoons of olive oil and the white wine. Add the garlic and sauté over low heat for about 10 minutes.

Meanwhile, heat the remaining olive oil and butter in a large pan. Add leeks and celery, and sauté until wilted, about 10 minutes. Add the beans and yuca or potato to the leeks with the chicken stock, herbs, and bay leaves. Add the garlic mixture and simmer until the yuca or potato is soft, about 30 minutes. Remove the bay leaves. Add salt and pepper to taste. Purée in a blender or food processor. Garnish and serve immediately.

GARBANZO SOUP WITH RED PEPPER SALSA

Serves 6

Don't let the number of ingredients in this recipe put you off! It is a lightly spiced, creamy soup with a zingy salsa garnish—a real winner!

Ingredients

⅔ cup garbanzo, soaked overnight
1 tsp cumin seeds
½ tsp mustard seeds, preferably white
1 Tbsp sesame seeds
1 large onion, sliced fine
1 Tbsp olive oil
2 large garlic cloves, sliced fine
½ tsp ground ginger
3¼ cups well-flavored vegetable stock
Salt and ground black pepper
1¼ cups milk

For the salsa

½ small red bell pepper, chopped
¼ cucumber, chopped
½ small red onion, chopped fine
1 garlic clove, chopped fine
1 tomato, chopped
1 small red chile, seeded and chopped fine
1–2 Tbsp cilantro leaves, torn
Shredded rind and juice of 1 lemon
1–2 Tbsp sour cream (optional)

Drain the garbanzos and rinse them thoroughly under cold running water; set aside. Heat a non-stick frying pan until evenly hot, then add the cumin, mustard, and sesame seeds, and roast for 2 to 3 minutes, or until they start to pop. Transfer the spices to a mortar or a spice mill, and then grind until smooth. You may also use the end of a rolling pin to grind the spices.

Cook the onion in the oil in a large pan until well browned, then add the garlic, ginger, and freshly ground spices, and cook slowly for another minute. Stir in the garbanzos, and the stock, then bring the soup to a boil and season lightly. Simmer for 45 to 60 minutes, until the garbanzos are soft.

Prepare the salsa while the soup is cooking. Mix together all the prepared vegetables, season lightly, then add the cilantro, lemon rind, and lemon juice. Allow the salsa to stand for at least 30 minutes for the flavors to blend together.

Allow the soup to cool slightly, then purée until smooth in a blender or food processor. Rinse the pan and return the soup to it, then reheat gently with the milk, seasoning with salt and pepper to taste. Blend the salsa with 1 to 2 tablespoons of sour cream, if wished, then serve the soup in warm bowls with a generous spoonful of salsa in each portion.

CHICKEN AND BEAN SOUP

Serves 6

This is based on an Italian recipe for a tomato and bean soup.

Ingredients

2 Tbsp olive oil

2 chicken thighs

1 large onion, chopped fine

1 green bell pepper, cut into strips

1 red chile, seeded and chopped fine

2 garlic cloves, minced

1 Tbsp chopped fresh oregano

1 Tbsp Italian parsley

14-oz can chopped tomatoes

2 Tbsp tomato paste

2¾ pt chicken or vegetable stock

Salt and ground black pepper

15-oz tin borlotti beans or mixed pulses, drained and rinsed

Chopped fresh parsley and Parmesan cheese, to garnish

Heat the oil in a large pan; add the chicken and brown all over. Remove the chicken from the pan with a slotted spoon and set aside. Stir the onion into the pan juices and cook until softened but not browned. Add the pepper, chile, and garlic with the herbs and stir well. Add the tomatoes, tomato paste, and stock, then return the chicken to the pan, season, and bring the soup to a boil. Cover and simmer for 40 to 50 minutes, until the chicken is cooked.

Remove the chicken from the pan and take the meat from the bones. Shred the chicken and return it to the pan with the beans. Return the soup to a boil, then simmer for 3 to 4 minutes to heat the beans thoroughly.

Season the soup to taste, then garnish with chopped parsley. Slivers of Parmesan cheese may be sprinkled into the soup before serving.

FAVA BEAN AND PARSNIP SOUP

Serves 6

Ingredients

1 onion, chopped

2 Tbsp oil

1 garlic clove

1 cup diced parsnip

7 oz dried fava beans, soaked overnight

4¼ cups well-flavored vegetable stock

Salt and ground black pepper

Freshly grated nutmeg

1 cup milk

For the croutons

2 slices whole-wheat bread

2 Tbsp butter

1 Tbsp chopped fresh parsley

Cook the onion in the oil, add the garlic and parsnip, and continue cooking until the parsnip starts to brown.

Drain the soaked fava beans and rinse them thoroughly. Add the beans to the pan with the stock, some salt, pepper, and nutmeg. Bring the soup to a boil, then cover and simmer for about an hour, until the beans are tender.

Allow the soup to cool slightly then purée it in a blender. Rinse the pan and return the soup to it with the milk. Heat while preparing the croutons.

Toast the bread on one side only. Beat the butter with salt and pepper and the parsley. Spread the mixture over the untoasted side of the bread and cook until browned. Trim away the crusts, then cut the bread into squares.

Season the soup to taste, then serve garnished with the croutons.

◀ *Chicken and Bean Soup*

SEAFOOD SOUPS

SMOKED SALMON CHOWDER

Serves 6

Ingredients

1 Tbsp butter

3–4 shallots, chopped fine

2 celery stalks, chopped fine

5 cups water

1 bay leaf

2 salmon steaks (about 1 lb total weight)

2 potatoes (about 1 lb), diced

1¼ cups light cream

Ground black pepper

7 oz smoked salmon, cut in small pieces

1 Tbsp chopped fresh dill

1 Tbsp snipped fresh chives

Melt the butter in a heavy pan over medium-low heat. Add the shallots and celery, and sweat until slightly softened. Add the water and bay leaf, cover, and simmer gently for 10 minutes.

Add the salmon steaks and poach for 10 minutes over low heat, covered. Transfer to a plate and allow the fish to cool slightly. Discard the salmon skin and bones, and flake the flesh coarsely.

Meanwhile, stir the potatoes into the cooking liquid and simmer for 15 to 20 minutes, partially covered, until they are tender.

Add the cream to the chowder, season with pepper, and simmer for about 5 minutes to heat through. Stir in the poached salmon, smoked salmon pieces, and herbs, and continue cooking for 5 minutes. Taste and adjust the seasoning, and ladle into warm soup plates or bowls. Serve with fresh bread.

CREAMY MUSSEL SOUP

Serves 4

Ingredients

4½ lb fresh mussels

⅔ cup dry white wine

Bouquet garni (thyme sprigs, parsley, and bay leaf)

Ground black pepper

1 tsp butter

2 large shallots, chopped fine

1 carrot, diced fine

1¼ cups heavy cream

1 Tbsp cornstarch dissolved in water

2 Tbsp chopped fresh parsley

Discard any broken mussels and those with open shells that refuse to close when tapped. Remove any barnacles and pull out the stringy "beards." Rinse in several changes of cold water.

In a large heavy pan combine the wine, *bouquet garni*, and pepper. Bring to a boil and cook for 2 minutes. Add the mussels, cover, and cook for 5 minutes, or until the mussels open, shaking the pan occasionally.

When they are cool, remove the mussels from the shells, straining any juices into the cooking liquid. Strain the cooking liquid through a strainer lined with damp cheesecloth.

Melt the butter in a pan. Add the shallots and carrot, and cook until the shallots are soft. Stir in the mussel cooking liquid and bring to a boil. Reduce the heat to low and simmer until the vegetables are tender, about 30 minutes.

Add the cream and bring just to a boil. Stir the cornstarch mixture to combine, and stir it into the soup. Boil for 2 to 3 minutes until thickened, stirring frequently. Add the mussels and cook for 1 to 2 minutes longer to reheat them. Stir in the parsley and ladle into a warm tureen or soup bowls.

Smoked Salmon Chowder ▶

SQUID, PUMPKIN, AND TOMATO SOUP

Serves 4

Squid should be cooked very briefly to avoid it becoming chewy.

Ingredients

1 large onion, chopped fine
3 Tbsp extra virgin olive oil
3 cups peeled, seeded, and diced pumpkin
1 lb prepared squid rings
2 garlic cloves, sliced fine
2 tsp paprika
2 cups puréed tomatoes or thick tomato juice
1 cup fish or vegetable stock
2 bay leaves
Salt and ground black pepper
Light cream and chopped fresh parsley, to garnish

Cook the onion for 5 to 6 minutes in the oil in a large pan over low heat, until softened but not browned. Add the pumpkin, continue to cook for 3 to 4 minutes, then stir in the squid. Increase the heat and cook for 2 to 3 minutes, until the squid is opaque, then add the garlic and paprika. Lower the heat and continue cooking for a further 2 to 3 minutes.

Add the puréed tomatoes or tomato juice, the stock, and bay leaves. Season well, then bring the soup slowly to a boil. Cover, and cook over very low heat for 1½ to 2 hours, stirring occasionally.

Remove the bay leaves, then adjust the seasoning if necessary. Add a little water if the soup has become too thick.

Serve in warmed bowls with a swirl of cream and a scattering of freshly chopped parsley.

POTATO AND FISH SOUP

Serves 4–6

Ingredients

1–2 small fish (such as red mullet or sole), scaled and filleted
About 3 cups water
1½ lb new potatoes
½ tsp salt
1¼ cups mayonnaise
2 Tbsp wine vinegar
For fish stock (optional)
Heads from 1 lb shrimp
1 celery stalk, chopped
A few parsley stalks
1 bay leaf

Put the bones and heads from the fish, plus the other ingredients for the fish stock in a pan with the water. Simmer for about 25 minutes, while you peel and dice the potatoes.

Strain the stock, return to the pan, and add the potatoes and salt. Cook until tender, then add the fish, in small pieces, for the last 5 minutes. Remove the potatoes and fish to a serving bowl.

Let the stock cool a little. Stir the stock into the mayonnaise, to make a creamy soup and pour over the potatoes and fish. Check the seasoning, stir in the vinegar, and serve warm. Pass a jug of vinegar round the table, if you wish.

◄ *Squid, Pumpkin, and Tomato Soup*

CATALAN MUSSEL SOUP

Serves 4

This is one of the best Spanish mussel soups, which has a hint of anis, *though a big glass of dry white wine can replace the spirits.*

Ingredients

2 lb fresh mussels
2 Tbsp olive oil
1 mild Spanish onion, chopped
1 garlic clove, chopped fine
2 large, ripe tomatoes, skinned, seeded, and chopped
½ cup anis, *aguadiente* (or Pernod)
Salt and ground black pepper
A pinch of cayenne pepper
Juice of ½ lemon
2 Tbsp chopped fresh parsley
4 slices of stale bread

Clean the mussels. Cover them with cold water then scrub them one by one. Pull off all the "beards." Throw out any that are broken or do not close when tapped.

Meanwhile, heat the oil in a pan large enough to contain all the ingredients and fry the onion gently, adding the garlic when it softens. Add the chopped tomato flesh and juice to the pan and cook until reduced to a sauce. Add ⅔ cup water to the pan.

Add the mussels in two or three batches. Cook with the lid on for 3 to 4 minutes until they open. Then use a slotted spoon to remove them to a plate and discard the top shell of each one. Throw away any that remain closed. When they are all done, return them to the pan and sprinkle with the *anis* or Pernod.

Add more water—about 1⅓ cups, and bring back to simmering. Season with salt and pepper, adding cayenne pepper, lemon juice to taste, and parsley. Break a slice of bread into the bottom of each bowl and ladle in the soup.

SHRIMP BISQUE

Serves 6

This soup should really need no salt added to it because of the tasty stock.

Ingredients

1 lb shrimp shells
5 Tbsp butter
1 small carrot
1 medium onion
1 bay leaf
4 Tbsp chopped fresh parsley
¼ cup brandy
Good ½ cup flour
5 Tbsp tomato paste
⅔ cup heavy cream

Boil the shrimp shells for 1 hour in just over 3 pints of unsalted water. In the meantime, melt the butter in a 4½-cup pan over low heat. Add the carrot and the onion, chopped very finely, the bay leaf, and the parsley, and stew very gently for about 10 minutes. Add the brandy and remove from the heat.

After 1 hour, strain the shrimp shells and top up the stock with water up to a quantity of 5 cups.

Add the flour to the butter, vegetables, and brandy mixture and cook gently for 3 to 4 minutes. Slowly add the shell stock and bring the liquid to a boil.

Add the tomato paste and then liquidize the mixture in a blender or food processor, or force through a fine strainer. Return the mixture to the heat, whisk in the cream and serve immediately.

PROVENÇAL FISH SOUP

Serves 6

Ingredients

1 lb white fish trimmings
1 large onion
2 Tbsp chopped fresh parsley
2 bay leaves
Juice of 1 lemon
1 Tbsp white wine
10 white peppercorns
¾ cup tomato paste
2 Tbsp paprika
A pinch saffron or turmeric
Salt and ground black pepper, to taste

Put the fish, the onion, peeled and halved, the parsley, bay leaves, lemon juice, and wine into 5 pints water and bring to a boil. Turn down the heat and simmer gently for 25 to 30 minutes.

Add the peppercorns and let the stock stand for 5 minutes or so. Strain, discard all the debris, and replace the stock on high heat.

Add the tomato paste, paprika, and saffron or turmeric. Reduce the stock by one third. Season to taste with salt and pepper. This soup can be made ahead and reheated—this also gives the flavors time to combine and mature.

Cook's tip

This soup is traditionally served with three accompaniments. They are: *Rouille*, a mayonnaise strongly flavored with cayenne pepper and garlic and colored with paprika; toasted baguette; and shredded Gruyère cheese.

OYSTER STEW

Serves 4

Essentially oysters cooked in cream, this rich 'stew' is deceptively easy.

Ingredients

25 g/4 oz butter
4 spring onions, finely chopped
25 g/1 oz celery, finely chopped
1.2 litres/2 pints single cream
½ tsp salt
¼ tsp cayenne pepper
2 tsp Worcestershire sauce
3 dozen large or 4 dozen small-medium oysters with their liquor, large oysters halved
Butter or sherry, to garnish

In a medium pan over low heat, melt the butter. Sauté the spring onions and celery until limp, about 5 minutes.

Add the single cream, salt, cayenne and Worcestershire sauce and heat until the soup just starts to boil. Lower the heat, add the oysters and their liquor and cook just until the edges of the oysters start to curl, 2 to 3 minutes. Taste and adjust the seasonings.

Garnish each bowl with a pat of butter or a dash of sherry.

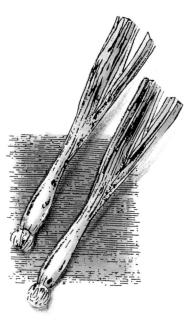

COCONUT SHRIMP SOUP

Serves 4

Ingredients

1 red bell pepper, diced

1½ Tbsp chopped scallions, including a small amount of green tops

2 cups homemade chicken stock or canned, with fat strained out

2 tsp chopped garlic

1 Tbsp grated fresh ginger root

1 Tbsp ground coriander

½ Tbsp curry powder

½ tsp dried thyme

½ tsp white pepper

½ tsp hot pepper sauce

1¾ cups coconut milk

1¼ lb medium shrimp, shelled and deveined

1 cup heavy cream

In a small bowl, mix together the red bell pepper and chopped scallions, and set aside.

In a 4-quart Dutch oven or pan over medium-high heat, bring the chicken stock, garlic, ginger, coriander, curry powder, thyme, pepper, hot pepper sauce, and coconut milk to a boil. Reduce the heat immediately and simmer for 5 minutes. Remove from the heat and skim any fat off the top.

Return to medium-high heat, bring to a simmer, and add half the red bell pepper and scallion mixture, and the shrimp. Simmer just until the shrimp is done, about 5 minutes. Do not overcook.

Remove from the heat and stir in the cream. Taste and adjust the seasoning. Ladle into warmed bowls, and garnish with the remaining red bell pepper and scallion mixture. Serve immediately with warm fresh bread.

CLAM AND ZUCCHINI SOUP

Serves 4

The recipe for this delicious soup comes from the Portuguese coast.

Ingredients

1½ lb baby clams, cleaned

1 plump garlic clove, chopped fine

3 Tbsp olive oil

1½ lb zucchini, sliced thick

Finely shredded rind of 1 small lemon, plus a squeeze of juice

1 Tbsp chopped fresh cilantro

4¼ cups fish or vegetable stock or water

Salt and ground black pepper

To serve

4 thick slices country bread, toasted

1 plump garlic clove, lightly crushed

Olive oil

Put the clams into a large pan, cover, and heat gently until the shells open. Reserve the juice and shell half the clams; reserve the other half for garnish.

Fry the garlic in the oil until softened and lightly colored; do not allow it to darken. Stir in the zucchini, lemon rind, and cilantro; then add the stock or water. Bring to a boil, cover, and simmer for 10 to 15 minutes until the zucchini are very tender.

Purée the soup in a blender or food processor, or pass through a food mill. Return to the pan and add the opened clams and reserved juice. Reheat gently without allowing the soup to boil as this would toughen the clams. Add the lemon juice and seasoning to taste.

To serve, rub the toasted bread with the garlic and place a slice in each of four warmed soup bowls. Pour over the soup, sprinkle with olive oil, and serve.

SHELLFISH BISQUE

Serves 4

In this Cajun recipe, crayfish are typically used, but virtually any kind of shellfish is suitable—small shrimp, crabs or lobsters, or use a mixture if you wish. Most of the flavor comes from the shells, so you could even make this soup after you have eaten the lobster!

Ingredients

12 oz small cooked shrimp in the shell, or 1 lb with heads, or about 1½ lb hard-shelled shellfish, such as crabs, crayfish, or lobster, cooked

2 Tbsp butter

4 Tbsp flour

2 Tbsp Cognac

A pinch of cayenne pepper

4–5 Tbsp heavy cream

Lemon juice

For the stock

2 tsp vegetable oil

Shellfish shells and heads, or chopped small shellfish (about 1 lb)

1 onion, halved and sliced

1 small carrot, sliced

1 celery stalk, sliced

4 cups water

½ lemon (unwaxed or scrubbed), sliced

Bouquet garni (thyme sprigs, parsley, and bay leaf)

Remove the shells and heads, if any, from the shrimp, reserving them for the stock. For crab, crayfish, or lobster, chop the shells in small pieces. Cover and chill the shellfish meat, either for use in the soup or for another purpose.

For the stock, heat the oil in a large pan over high heat. Add the shellfish shells and heads, if any, and sauté until they start to brown. Reduce the heat to medium and add the onion, carrot, and celery. Cook, stirring occasionally, for about 3 minutes, until the onion starts to soften. Add the water, lemon, and *bouquet garni*. Bring to a boil, reduce the heat to low, and simmer gently, partially covered, for 25 minutes. Strain the stock.

Melt the butter in a heavy pan over moderate heat. Then stir in the flour and cook until slightly golden, stirring occasionally. Add the Cognac and gradually pour in about half the stock, whisking vigorously until smooth, then add the remaining stock, still whisking. Season with cayenne pepper (salt is not usually needed). Reduce the heat, cover and simmer gently for about 5 minutes, stirring occasionally.

Strain the soup if not completely smooth. Add the cream and lemon juice to taste. Reheat the shellfish meat, if using, briefly in the soup before serving.

Cook's tip

If you have bought raw shellfish, cook it in boiling water and use the cooking water to make the stock. If using tiny crabs, the task of extracting any meat is too arduous, but chop them and cook as for shells.

SQUID WITH BELL PEPPERS AND TOMATO

Serves 4

Cook the squid gently so that it is not irrevocably toughened.

Ingredients

2¼ lb prepared squid

½ cup olive oil

2 onions, chopped fine

1 garlic clove, crushed

2 red bell peppers, cored, seeded, and sliced

1 lb well-flavored tomatoes, chopped

1 cup fish stock

6 Tbsp dry white wine

Salt and ground black pepper

2 slices country bread, toasted

1 Tbsp chopped fresh parsley

Cut the squid open into two halves; then cut across into 1-inch slices.

Heat the oil in a flameproof casserole. Add the onions, garlic, and bell peppers, and cook until softened. Stir in the tomatoes and bubble until well-blended and lightly thickened. Add the stock and wine, bring to a boil, and then lower the heat. Add the squid and seasoning, cover, and cook gently for 1 to 1½ hours, or until the squid is tender and the cooking juices have reduced to a light sauce; if necessary, remove the lid towards the end of cooking to allow the sauce to evaporate slightly.

Toast the bread, cut the slices in half, and put into a warmed, deep serving dish. Pour over the squid mixture and sprinkle with parsley, and serve immediately.

MUSSEL AND PINEAPPLE CURRY SOUP

Serves 4

Ingredients

4½ cups thin coconut milk

1 quantity chili paste

7 oz cooked mussel meat (steam 1½ lb mussels in their shells and remove meat)

½ medium-sized pineapple, finely diced

1 kaffir lime leaf, torn into small pieces

2½ Tbsp fish sauce

½ Tbsp sugar

For the chili paste

5 dried red chiles, chopped rough

1½ Tbsp sliced shallot

½ Tbsp finely sliced lemon grass

½ Tbsp garlic, chopped

2 tsp salt

1 tsp shrimp paste

1 tsp sliced galangal

½ tsp chopped kaffir lime zest

½ tsp chopped coriander root or stem

Pound all the chili paste ingredients together with a mortar and pestle or in a blender to form a fine paste.

Heat a quarter of the coconut milk in a pan, add the chili paste, and cook for 2 minutes. Add the mussels, mix thoroughly, then add the rest of the ingredients and boil for 1 minute.

Remove from the heat and serve in bowls accompanied by bread.

◀ *Squid with Bell Peppers and Tomato*

SHERRIED LOBSTER BISQUE

Serves 4–6

This is a rich, delectable soup. Use angler-fish, commonly called monkfish, if you can, because it tastes like more expensive lobster when cooked in this dish. But any firm-fleshed fish, such as red-fish, red snapper, tilefish, catfish, or cod, will do. Pair this soup with a green salad and some crusty bread and you have a memorable meal.

Ingredients

3 Tbsp butter
10–12 celery stalks, chopped
1 onion, chopped
¼ tsp dried thyme
½ tsp red pepper flakes
1 Tbsp fresh lemon zest
3 Tbsp self-rising flour
1⅓ cups chicken stock
1⅓ cups milk
1 lb lobster meat or substitute
2 Tbsp dry sherry
Salt and ground white pepper
1 Tbsp sweet red bell pepper slivers, to garnish
A pinch paprika, to garnish

In a large pan, melt the butter. Add the celery, onion, thyme, pepper flakes, and lemon zest. Cook until the vegetables are softened, stirring once, for about 20 minutes. Stir in the flour a little at a time. Gradually stir in the stock and milk. Cover and simmer until just bubbling and thick, stirring occasionally, about 5 to 10 minutes.

Add the seafood or fish, cover and cook until the fish is opaque, about 5 minutes. Season with sherry, salt, and pepper. Garnish lightly with bell peppers and paprika.

LEEK AND MUSSEL SOUP

Serves 4

Ingredients

5 pt fresh mussels
4 leeks
2 shallots
2 garlic cloves
3 Tbsp chopped fresh parsley
1 Tbsp chopped fresh dill
1 Tbsp snipped fresh chives
Half bottle dry white wine
1 stick butter, cut into small cubes
5 cups fish stock
A small pinch of saffron soaked in water
Ground black pepper

Prepare the mussels by removing the beards and any barnacles. Scrub well and rinse in clean water. Throw away any mussels that are broken or remain open when tapped. Place in a pan.

Chop the leeks, shallots, and garlic finely. Put in a pan with the parsley, dill, and chives.

Pour the wine over the clean mussels. Place on high heat until the mussels are steamed open. Discard any mussels that remain firmly closed. Take out the mussels, shell, and reserve. Reserve the liquor. Whip the butter cubes into the liquor.

Add the fish stock to the pan. Stir in the soaked saffron strands, simmer gently over low heat for a few minutes, and season with black pepper.

Add the shelled mussels and heat in the liquor but do not boil, as the mussels will get leathery.

Serve the soup in warm bowls garnished with more snipped chives and parsley. Serve with warm bread.

HOT AND SOUR NOODLE SOUP WITH SHRIMP

Serves 4

This is one of the representative dishes of Thai cuisine. The broth is a myriad of flavors: the sour element of lime leaves and lemon grass combined with the hot chile pepper and fish sauce, with its strong seafood aroma.

Ingredients

1 Tbsp vegetable oil
2 garlic cloves, minced
2 shallots, shredded
1-inch piece galangal, or ½-inch piece fresh ginger root, sliced thin
4–5 small red chiles, chopped
6 cups light chicken stock (see page 15)
3 kaffir lime leaves, sliced
4-inch piece lemon grass, chopped
½ lb rice vermicelli
20 peeled tiger shrimp
6 Tbsp fish sauce
6 Tbsp fresh lemon or lime juice
2 Tbsp brown sugar
16 canned straw mushrooms
Cilantro leaves

Heat the oil in a pan, then stir-fry the garlic, shallots, galangal or ginger, and chile for about 1 minute. Add the chicken stock, lime leaves, and lemon grass, bring to a boil, and simmer for 5 minutes.

Meanwhile, soak the rice vermicelli for 3 minutes, rinse, drain, and divide into four bowls. Add the shrimp, fish sauce, lemon or lime juice, sugar, and straw mushrooms to the soup, then simmer for 2 to 3 minutes.

Pour the soup into the bowls and sprinkle with the cilantro leaves. Serve immediately whilst piping hot.

SMOKED FISH SOUP

Serves 4–6

Ingredients

4½ cups chicken stock
½ oz galangal, sliced
2 lemon grass stalks, cut into 1½-inch pieces and crushed lightly
1 tsp shrimp paste
9 oz smoked fish (not salted), bones removed and broken into 3 or 4
1 oz shallots, crushed slightly
1½ tsp tamarind or lime juice, or to taste
½ cup sweet basil leaves
1 Tbsp fish sauce, or to taste
½ tsp salt
5 dried whole red chiles, dry-fried for 3–5 minutes

Pour the chicken stock into a pan, bring to a boil, and add the galangal, lemon grass, and shrimp paste. Boil again for 2 minutes and then add the dried fish pieces, shallot, and tamarind juice. Bring back to a boil, and simmer for 5 minutes, then remove from the heat and add the rest of the ingredients. Mix and season to taste with more tamarind, lime juice, or fish sauce if you like.

Stand for 10 minutes before serving. Serve accompanied by rice.

Hot and Sour Noodle Soup with Shrimp ▶

ROASTED PUMPKIN AND SMOKED MUSSEL SOUP

Serves 6

A luxurious soup that is just as good for a lazy lunch or as a sophisticated appetizer.

Ingredients

½ small pumpkin or 1 medium firm-fleshed squash (about 1 lb)

Salt and ground black pepper

3 Tbsp olive oil

1 leek, sliced fine

2 celery stalks, trimmed and sliced

1 carrot, sliced

2 tsp ground coriander

3–4 sprigs fresh thyme

1 bay leaf

3 cups well-flavored vegetable stock

1¾ cups milk

5½ oz smoked mussels

Preheat a 425°F oven. Cut the pumpkin or squash into slices about 1½ to 2 inches wide and place them in a roasting pan. You will need 6 slices. Season lightly with pepper then brush the flesh with olive oil. Bake in the preheated oven for about 30 minutes, until tender. Scoop the flesh from the skin and place to one side.

Heat 2 tablespoons of olive oil in a large pan; add the leek, celery, and carrot, and cook slowly for a further minute. Add the pumpkin or squash flesh to the pan with the coriander, thyme and bay leaf, then pour in the stock. Bring the soup to a boil, then cover, and simmer slowly for 35 to 40 minutes.

Allow the soup to cool slightly then purée until smooth in a blender or food processor. Rinse the pan then return the soup to it with the milk and bring slowly to simmering point. Season well with salt and pepper, then add the smoked mussels, and heat for another minute or two. Serve garnished with parsley, and warm bread.

BLACK AND WHITE SQUID SOUP

Serves 4

Ingredients

12 oz prepared squid, cut into thin rings

Juice of 1 lemon

3 oz squid ink pasta

4 cups fish or shellfish stock

A pinch of saffron threads, soaked in 3 Tbsp boiling water

Salt and white pepper

Put the squid in a nonreactive pan with the lemon juice and water to cover generously. Bring to a boil, reduce the heat to low, and simmer, partially covered, until the squid is tender, up to 1½ hours, adding more water if needed.

Bring a moderately large pan of salted water to a boil, add the pasta, and cook until tender but still a little chewy, *al dente*. Drain and rinse under cold running water.

Bring the stock to a boil, strain in the saffron water, and season with salt if needed and pepper to taste. Add the squid and pasta, and simmer for about 5 minutes until heated through. Ladle into a warm tureen or bowl.

Roasted Pumpkin and Smoked Mussel Soup ▶

ITALIAN FISH SOUP

Serves 6–8

Like bouillabaisse, *its counterpart in France, Italian* brodetto *has innumerable variations. What distinguishes* brodetto *is braising the onions in vinegar for the soup base. Use several kinds of firm white-fleshed fish and avoid particularly oily ones. According to tradition, the fish should not be too "noble"—this is the food of fishermen.*

Ingredients

2 Tbsp olive oil

2 onions, chopped

5 Tbsp white wine vinegar

2 garlic cloves, chopped fine

1 carrot, shredded

1 lb ripe tomatoes, peeled, seeded, and chopped, or 1¾ cups canned chopped Italian tomatoes in juice

2 cups dry white wine

2 Tbsp tomato paste

1½ cups fish stock or 1 cup water

8 oz prepared squid, cut into rings

Shredded zest of 1 lemon (unwaxed or scrubbed)

1 bay leaf

2 lb white fish fillets, such as red snapper, cod, haddock, monkfish, shark, or swordfish, skinned if wished and cut into pieces

1 lb small clams, scrubbed

2 Tbsp chopped fresh parsley

For the garlic croutons (see page 188)

Heat the oil in a large heavy pan or flameproof casserole over medium heat. Add the onions and cook until softened, about 3 minutes. Add the vinegar and cook, stirring frequently, until the vinegar has evaporated and continue cooking until the onions are golden.

Add the garlic and carrot to the onion mixture, cook for 2 to 3 minutes and stir in the tomatoes and wine. Bring to a boil and boil for 1 minute. Stir in the tomato paste, stock or water, and the squid, lemon zest, and bay leaf. Reduce the heat to low and simmer, partially covered, until the squid is tender, about 30 minutes, stirring occasionally.

Arrange the thicker pieces of fish over the mixture and push them into the soup. Put the thinner pieces of fish and the clams over the top, cover, and continue simmering for about 5 minutes longer, or until the fish is opaque throughout and the clams have opened. Ladle into a warm tureen or bowls, sprinkle with parsley and serve with garlic croutons.

Cook's tip

The soup may be prepared several hours in advance except for adding the fish and shellfish. Allow to cool, cover, and chill. Reheat to simmering before continuing with step 3. If you wish, omit the squid and clams, and use only white fish, increasing the amount to about 2½ pounds.

RAMEN WITH CRAB OMELET

Serves 4

Typically, crab omelet is served on its own. The inspiration behind the dish is Chinese, but the Japanese have a preference for it served on a bowl of noodles.

Ingredients

1 lb *ramen* noodles, or 14 oz fresh *or* ¾ lb dried thin egg noodles

6 cups soy sauce broth (see page 15)

For the omelet

6 eggs

6 oz canned crab meat

4 shiitake mushrooms, sliced

2 scallions, sliced thin

4 Tbsp canned bamboo shoots, sliced thin

Salt and white pepper

2–3 Tbsp vegetable oil

1 chopped scallion, to garnish

First, to make the omelet, put the eggs, crab meat, mushrooms, scallion, and bamboo shoots in a bowl. Season with salt and pepper, and mix.

Heat the oil in a frying pan or wok until very hot. Pour in the egg mixture, and heat for 30 seconds. Stir lightly with chopsticks or a spatula a few times. When it is nearly set, turn it over. The mixture should be soft like scrambled eggs, but be cooked just enough to be able to retain the shape of an omelet.

Boil plenty of water in a large pan. Add the noodles and cook over a high heat for 3 minutes, or according to the instructions on the package. Drain, then divide among four bowls.

Heat the soy sauce broth. Place the crab meat on the noodles and pour the broth over the top. Sprinkle with the chopped scallion and serve.

MEDITERRANEAN FISH SOUP

Serves 8

Many versions of this soup, Bouillabaisse, *can be found along the Mediterranean coast. Almost any combination of fish and shellfish can be used, but strongly-flavored oily fish are best avoided.*

Ingredients

3 lb firm white fish fillets, such as sea bass, snapper, and monkfish
3 Tbsp olive oil
Shredded zest of 1 orange (unwaxed or scrubbed)
1 garlic clove, minced
A pinch of saffron threads
2 Tbsp Pernod
1½ lb large shrimp
1 small fennel bulb, chopped fine
1 large onion, chopped fine
8 oz small new potatoes, sliced
12 oz sea scallops, rinsed
Croutons (see page 188)
Rouille (see page 190)

For the stock

2–3 lb fish heads, bones, and trimmings
2 Tbsp olive oil
2 leeks, sliced
1 onion, halved and sliced
1 red bell pepper, cored and sliced
1½ lb ripe tomatoes, cored and quartered
4 garlic cloves, sliced
Bouquet garni (thyme sprigs, parsley, and bay leaf)
Rind of 1 orange (unwaxed or scrubbed), removed with a vegetable peeler
2–3 pinches saffron threads
4 pt water

Cut the fish fillets into bite-sized pieces. Trim off any thin ragged bits and reserve for the stock. Put the fish into a large bowl with 2 tablespoons of the olive oil, the orange zest, garlic, saffron, and Pernod. Turn to coat well. Peel the shrimp and reserve the shells. Cover and chill the shrimp and the fish separately.

For the stock, rinse the fish heads, bones, and trimmings under cold running water to remove any blood. Heat the olive oil in a large nonreactive pan or flameproof casserole. Add the leeks, onion, and bell pepper, and cook over medium heat, stirring occasionally, until the onion starts to soften, about 5 minutes.

Add the reserved shrimp shells, fish heads, bones, and trimmings, and continue cooking for 2 minutes. Stir in the tomatoes, garlic, *bouquet garni*, orange zest, saffron, and water (top up if necessary to cover the ingredients). Bring to a boil, skimming off the foam as it rises, then reduce the heat, and simmer gently, covered, for 30 minutes, skimming once or twice. Strain the stock.

To finish the fish soup, heat the remaining tablespoon of olive oil in a deep sauté pan or wide flameproof casserole over medium heat. Cook the chopped fennel and onion until the onion starts to soften, about 5 minutes, then add the strained stock. Bring to a boil, add the potatoes, and cook for 5 minutes.

Reduce the heat to medium-low and add the fish, starting with the thickest pieces and putting in the thinner ones after 2 to 3 minutes. Add the shrimp and scallops, and continue simmering gently until all the seafood is cooked (opaque throughout).

Transfer the fish, shellfish, and potatoes to a warm tureen or soup plates. Taste for seasoning and ladle the soup over. Serve with croutons spread with *rouille*.

Cook's tip

You can prepare the *rouille* and croutons in advance and make the stock for the soup early in the day while the fish fillets marinate. Then the final assembly isn't too difficult.

SHRIMP AND LEEK BISQUE

Serves 6

This rich, creamy bisque starts with a flavorful shrimp stock. It's important to make your own stock for this soup, so it picks up the delicate flavor of leeks. If you can't find shrimp with heads, get some extra shells to make the stock with. You can make the soup, up to the point of puréeing, early in the day, then reheat and add the cream just before serving.

Ingredients

³⁄₄ lb medium shrimp, shelled and deveined with heads and shells reserved
1 large carrot, unpeeled, cut into chunks
2 celery stalks, leaves and all, sliced
2 leeks, including green tops, sliced
2–3 sprigs of fresh parsley
2 bay leaves
5 black peppercorns
3 Tbsp butter
1 leek, white part only, chopped
2 garlic cloves, minced
3 cups sliced mushrooms
2 Tbsp minced fresh parsley
1 bay leaf
1 tsp salt
2 tsp chopped fresh basil
1 tsp chopped fresh thyme
¹⁄₈ tsp each black, white, and cayenne pepper
¹⁄₂ tsp dry mustard
3 Tbsp flour
1¹⁄₂ cups heavy cream
2 Tbsp sherry

Put the shrimp heads and shells, carrot, celery, leeks, parsley, bay leaves, and peppercorns in a large pan. Add 1 quart water. Make a mental note of the water level in the pot, because you will want to have at least 1 quart of stock after it has simmered for several hours. Add another 1 to 2 quarts water, enough to cover the shrimp shells and vegetables by several inches. Bring to a full boil. Skim off the gray foam. Reduce the heat and simmer, uncovered, for 2 to 3 hours, adding extra water if necessary to keep at least 1 quart of liquid in the pan.

Strain the stock, discarding the shrimp heads, shells, and vegetables. Measure 1 quart stock into a small pan; freeze or chill any remaining stock for future use. Return 1 quart of stock to the stove and keep warm over low heat.

In a frying pan, melt the butter. Sauté the leek, garlic, and mushrooms about 10 minutes. Add the vegetables to the stock with the seasonings. Bring to a boil, then reduce the heat, and simmer, uncovered, 15 minutes. Add the shrimp and simmer just until shrimp are opaque and tightly curled.

Purée the soup in a blender or food processor; you will probably have to do this in several batches. (At this point you may wish to chill the puréed soup for several hours. Reheat before continuing.)

Whisk the flour into the cream, then add to the soup. Heat just short of boiling point. Taste and adjust the seasoning. Add the sherry.

CRAB-CORN CHOWDER

Serves 4

A favorite recipe, this soup has a wonderfully rich taste and makes an ideal lunch or light supper.

Ingredients

2 Tbsp butter
½ onion, chopped
1 celery stalk, chopped fine
1 garlic clove, minced
1½ cups shellfish stock (see page 12)
½ cup dry white wine or chicken stock (see page 12)
1 cup fresh or frozen corn kernels
¼ tsp dried thyme
½ tsp salt
A pinch cayenne pepper
¼ tsp white pepper
1 cup half-and-half
½ cup sour cream
½ lb crab meat
1 Tbsp chopped fresh parsley
2 scallions, chopped

In a large pan over low heat, melt the butter. Sauté the onion, celery, and garlic until wilted, about 5 minutes.

Add the shellfish stock and wine or chicken stock, and bring to a boil. Add the corn and spices. Return to a boil, then reduce the heat, and simmer, uncovered, about 20 minutes.

Stir in the half-and-half and continue simmering for 10 minutes but do not boil. Whisk in the sour cream. Add the crab meat, parsley, and scallions, and heat just enough to warm the crab. Do not allow to boil.

CHUNKY TUNISIAN FISH SOUP

Serves 6–8

This is a substantial fish soup. Any selection of fish and shellfish can be used except oily fish such as mackerel and sardines. If you like, you can use the heads, tails, skin, and bones to make fish stock for the soup.

Ingredients

3 Tbsp olive oil
2 onions, chopped
3 garlic cloves, chopped
1 red bell pepper, chopped
About 1 tsp Harissa (see below)
$\frac{1}{4}$ tsp crushed saffron threads
$\frac{1}{4}$–$\frac{1}{2}$ tsp ground cinnamon
$\frac{1}{4}$–$\frac{1}{2}$ tsp ground cumin
1 fennel bulb, diced, feathery fronds reserved
2 large potatoes, chopped
$2\frac{1}{2}$–3 Tbsp lemon juice
6 cups fish stock or water
$4\frac{1}{2}$ lb mixed fish and shellfish, prepared
4 well-flavored tomatoes, peeled, seeded, and chopped
1 large bunch of mixed cilantro and parsley, chopped fine
Salt and ground black pepper
Bread, to serve

Heat the oil in a large frying pan, then fry the onion until softened but not colored. Add the garlic and red bell pepper, cook for 2 to 3 minutes, then stir in the *Harissa*, spices, fennel, potatoes, lemon juice, and stock or water. Bring to a boil then simmer for about 20 minutes until the potatoes are almost cooked. Add the fish, tomatoes, herbs, seasoning, and water as necessary, and cook gently until the fish is tender.

Serve sprinkled with the reserved fennel fronds and accompanied by warmed crusty bread.

HARISSA

Or "arhissa" as it is sometimes called, is a fiery paste based on chiles. As well as being served as a condiment at the table, in a small dish with a small spoon, Harissa is used in cooking to add life to meat, poultry, or vegetable casseroles, saffron-flavored fish soups and stews, "stewed" red bell peppers, and tomatoes.

Ingredients

2 oz dried red chiles, soaked in hot water for 1 hour
2 garlic cloves, chopped
2 tsp coriander seeds
2 tsp cumin seeds
2 tsp caraway seeds
A pinch of salt
6 Tbsp olive oil

Drain the chiles and put in a mortar, spice grinder, or small blender with the garlic, spices, and salt. Mix to a paste then stir in 3 tablespoons of olive oil. Transfer to a small jar and pour a little oil over the surface. Cover and keep chilled for up to 2 to 3 days.

Chunky Tunisian Fish Soup ▶

ASIAN SCALLOP SOUP

Serves 4

This exotic soup is quick to prepare. Miso, *made from soya beans is used as a base for many different Asian soups.*

Ingredients

4 cups water
4 tsp *miso* (bean paste, available at health food stores)
3 oz shiitake mushrooms, stems removed
1 garlic clove, halved
1-inch piece lemon grass or peeled fresh ginger root
3–4 scallions, cut into julienne strips about 2 inches long
1 tsp light soy sauce, or to taste
1 tsp lemon juice, or to taste
6 large sea scallops, about 8 oz
Cilantro leaves, to garnish

Bring the water to a boil in a medium pan. Thin the *miso* with a little of the water, reduce the heat to low, and stir in the diluted *miso*.

Slice the mushrooms thinly and add to the *miso* broth with the garlic and lemon grass or ginger. Simmer gently for 10 to 12 minutes, or until the mushrooms are tender. Remove the garlic and lemon grass or ginger, and stir in the scallion strips. Season with soy sauce and lemon juice.

Pull off the coral from the scallops, if any, carefully. Discard the small hard muscle on the side and slice the scallops crosswise to form two or three thinner rounds from each. Simmer the scallops and corals in the broth until the flesh becomes opaque, 1 to 2 minutes.

Divide the scallop rounds among four warm bowls, ladle the soup over, and float a few cilantro leaves on each serving.

CURRIED CRAB SOUP

Serves 4–6

Female crabs are best for soup because the roe adds flavor and color.

Ingredients

5 Tbsp butter
1 shallot, chopped fine
4 Tbsp flour
½ tsp curry powder
2–3 Tbsp sherry
⅔ cup shellfish stock or bottled clam juice diluted with water
1 bay leaf
1¼ lb tomatoes, peeled, seeded, and chopped
1 cup light cream
8 oz crab meat, picked over (1¾ cups)
Tabasco sauce (optional)
4–6 crab claws, cracked and peeled, to garnish

Melt the butter in a pan over medium-low heat. Add the shallot and cook for about 5 minutes, stirring frequently. Stir in the flour and curry powder, and cook for 2 minutes. Add the sherry and cook, stirring constantly, until smooth and thick.

Gradually stir in the stock and add the bay leaf and tomatoes. Simmer, stirring occasionally, for about 15 minutes, until the vegetables are soft.

Work the soup through the medium blade of a food mill set over a bowl.

Stir in the cream and crab meat. Adjust the seasoning, and add a few drops of Tabasco sauce, if you wish. Ladle into bowls and garnish with crab claws.

OYSTERS IN PARSLEY AND GARLIC CREAM

Serves 4

The parsley in this creamy soup tames the garlic and gives it a brilliant color. It is delicious made with plump succulent oysters, but if you prefer, you can substitute cooked mussels or snails.

Ingredients

16–20 fresh oysters

1 large bunch of curly-leaf parsley, stems removed (about 6 cups leaves)

1½ cups heavy cream

1–2 garlic cloves, chopped fine

3–4 Tbsp shellfish stock or water (optional)

Salt and ground black pepper

1 ripe tomato (preferably plum), peeled, seeded, and diced

Working over a bowl to catch the juices, open the oysters: hold in a cloth (flat-side up), push the knife into the hinge, then work it around until you can pry off the top shell. When all the oysters have been opened, strain the liquid through a strainer lined with damp cheesecloth. Remove the oysters to the filtered liquid. (This may be done several hours in advance; chill, covered.)

Bring a large pan of salted water to a boil. Drop in the parsley leaves and cook for 3 to 4 minutes until bright green and tender. Drain and refresh in cold water. Press with the back of a spoon to extract as much water as possible. (This may be done up to 1 day in advance.)

Combine the cream and garlic in a medium pan and simmer over medium-low heat for 15 minutes until the garlic is tender and the cream has thickened slightly. Transfer to a blender or a food processor fitted with a steel blade, add the parsley, and purée until smooth. Return the purée to the pan and stir in the oyster liquid. If you wish, thin with shellfish stock or water.

Season to taste with salt, if needed, and pepper. Simmer the soup gently for about 5 minutes. Add the oysters and continue cooking for 1 to 2 minutes until the oysters are just heated through. Remove them with a slotted spoon and divide among four warm shallow soup plates. Ladle over the soup and garnish with diced tomato.

POULTRY AND GAME SOUPS

TARRAGON CHICKEN CONSOMME WITH CHICKEN QUENELLES

Serves 6

A richly flavored, sparkling clear consommé is considered a true indicator of culinary skill. Although it is relatively expensive and time-consuming, it is worth making the effort at least once.

Ingredients

1 skinless boneless chicken breast
2 small leeks, chopped fine
1 onion, chopped fine
1 celery stalk, chopped fine
3–4 sprigs of fresh parsley, chopped fine
2 tsp dried tarragon
2 egg whites
4 pt strong fat-free chicken stock
Chopped fresh tarragon leaves, to garnish

For the chicken quenelles

1 skinless boneless chicken breast, well chilled
1 egg white
1 Tbsp chopped fresh tarragon
4 Tbsp heavy cream, well chilled
Salt and ground black pepper
Freshly grated nutmeg

Finely chop the chicken breast in a food processor or by hand. Put in a large pan with the leeks, onion, celery, parsley, and dried tarragon. Add the egg whites, mix to combine and stir in the stock. Set over high heat and stir almost continuously as the mixture comes to a boil. When it begins to tremble, reduce the heat to low, and simmer very gently, without stirring or disturbing it, for 30 minutes. Carefully lift off about a third of the solid covering, using a slotted spoon, and ladle the clarified stock through a strainer lined with damp cheesecloth. (Discard the solid matter.)

For the chicken quenelles, cut the chicken breast into large pieces, put in a food processor fitted with a steel blade and process until smooth. Add the egg white and tarragon, and mix until combined. Add the cream by spoonfuls. Do not overprocess or the mixture will become warm and the cream will not be readily absorbed. Season generously and chill for at least 15 minutes.

Bring a pan of salted water to a simmer. Using two teaspoons, shape the chicken mixture into small ovals and drop into the water a few at a time. Poach for about 2 minutes until they float and feel firm to the touch. Drain on clean paper towels.

Bring the consommé just to a boil over medium-high heat. Divide the quenelles among warmed shallow soup plates, ladle over the consommé, and sprinkle with a little chopped tarragon. Serve immediately.

CABBAGE AND BEAN SOUP WITH PRESERVED DUCK OR GOOSE

Serves 8–10

This soup from Béarn, north of the Pyrenees, has many local and seasonal variations, such as the addition of Swiss chard or kale, chestnuts, or garlic sausage. It should be thick enough for a spoon to stand upright and is usually cooked in a special earthenware kettle.

Ingredients

2¼ cups dried white beans, soaked overnight
3–4 leg pieces preserved duck or goose (*confit*), with fat
2 onions, chopped fine
1 lb lean salt pork, rind removed, diced
5 pt duck or chicken stock, or water
8 oz boneless pork shoulder
Bouquet garni (parsley, thyme and marjoram sprigs, and bay leaf)
1 onion, studded with 3–4 cloves
2 leeks, halved lengthwise and sliced fine
2 carrots, sliced
2 white turnips, quartered
4 garlic cloves, minced
Salt and ground black pepper
1 medium green cabbage, quartered
3 potatoes, cubed
2 Tbsp chopped fresh parsley

To serve

8–10 large croutons (see page 188)
⅔ cup shredded Gruyère cheese

Drain the beans, put in a pan with cold water to cover, and set over high heat. Bring to a boil and boil for 10 minutes. Drain and add fresh cold water to cover. Bring to a boil again, drain, and rinse well.

Scrape the fat from the *confit* and reserve separately from the meat.

Heat 3 tablespoons of the fat from the *confit* in a large flameproof casserole over medium-high heat. Add the chopped onions and salt pork and cook until lightly browned, stirring frequently. Add the beans, stock, pork, *bouquet garni*, and studded onion. Simmer over low heat for 1 hour, skimming off the fat and stirring occasionally.

Add the leeks, carrots, turnips, and half the garlic and continue cooking for 20 minutes, or until the beans and meat are tender, stirring constantly. Taste and season with salt, if needed, and pepper.

Bring a large pan of salted water to a boil and add the cabbage. Cook, uncovered, for 10 minutes, rinse under cold water and drain.

Add the cabbage and potatoes to the beans with the cooked ham, the remaining garlic, and the parsley. Stir to combine and add the pieces of *confit*.

Continue simmering for 45 minutes, or until all the vegetables are tender.

Preheat a 400°F oven. If you wish, transfer the soup to an ovenproof tureen. Arrange the croutons over the top and sprinkle lightly with the shredded cheese. Place on the top shelf of the oven and bake until the top is browned, about 10 minutes.

SMOKED CHICKEN AND LENTIL SOUP

Serves 4

Lentils are often paired with smoked meats as they seem to give a pleasing element of richness.

Ingredients

1 Tbsp butter
2 leeks, split and sliced thin
2 carrots, chopped fine
1 large onion, chopped fine
1 garlic clove, minced
1 cup dried lentils (preferably *Puy*)
4 cups chicken stock
Bouquet garni (thyme sprigs, celery leaves, sage, and bay leaf)
1⅓ cups cubed smoked chicken
Salt and ground black pepper

Melt the butter in a large pan or stockpot over medium heat. Add the leeks, carrots, onion, and garlic, and cook for 4 to 5 minutes until slightly softened, stirring frequently.

Rinse and drain the lentils, and check for any small stones. Add to the vegetables with the stock and *bouquet garni*. Bring to a boil, reduce the heat to medium-low, and simmer for about 30 minutes, or until the lentils are just tender.

Add the chicken, season to taste with salt and pepper, and continue cooking for 15 minutes. Remove the *bouquet garni* and ladle into a warm tureen or bowls.

CHICKEN MINESTRONE

Serves 8–10

Ingredients

¾ cup dried cannellini or borlotti beans, soaked overnight
4 garlic cloves, minced
Bouquet garni (parsley stems, thyme sprigs, rosemary sprig, and bay leaf)
1 Tbsp olive oil
1 onion, chopped fine
5 pt chicken stock
2 cups cubed cooked chicken
3 cups diced pumpkin
1 leek, thinly sliced
2 sage leaves, finely chopped, or ¼ tsp dried
Salt and ground black pepper
4 cups broccoli rabe, leaves cut into ribbons, stems peeled and cut in ¾-inch pieces
3 small zucchini, halved lengthwise and sliced
1 cup small pasta shapes

Drain the beans, put in a pan with cold water to cover, and set over high heat. Bring to a boil and boil for 10 minutes. Drain, rinse, and return to the pan. Add half the garlic and the *bouquet garni*, and cover generously with fresh water. Bring to a boil, reduce the heat to low, and simmer until tender, 1 to 1½ hours, adding boiling water as needed to keep the beans covered by at least 1 inch. Discard the *bouquet garni*.

Heat the oil in a large heavy pan over medium heat and add the onion. Cook for 2 to 3 minutes until slightly softened, stirring occasionally, then add the remaining garlic and continue cooking for 2 minutes, stirring frequently. Add the stock, the beans and their cooking liquid, chicken, pumpkin, leek, and sage, and season to taste with salt and pepper. Bring to a boil, reduce the heat to medium-low, and simmer for 5 minutes. Stir in the broccoli rabe, zucchini, and pasta, and continue cooking for 15 to 20 minutes longer, or until the pasta and all the vegetables are tender.

Taste and adjust the seasoning, and ladle the soup into warm bowls.

Smoked Chicken and Lentil Soup ▶

THAI-SPICED CHICKEN CHOWDER

Serves 4

A spicy soup that is a meal in itself. Peel the outer skin from the lemon grass then flatten slightly with the blade of a knife before chopping fine.

Ingredients

1–2 Tbsp peanut or sunflower oil

2 small, boneless chicken breasts, skinned and shredded

2 tsp Thai 7-spice seasoning

1 stalk lemon grass, chopped fine

2 medium potatoes, diced

2⅔ cups chicken or vegetable stock

1¾ cups milk

3–4 scallions, trimmed and sliced fine

1 cup frozen peas

1–2 Tbsp satay sauce or peanut butter

Salt and ground black pepper

1–2 Tbsp heavy cream, to garnish

Heat the oil in a large pan; add the chicken and 7-spice and cook quickly until the chicken begins to brown. Stir in the lemon grass and potato, then add the liquids. Bring the chowder slowly to a boil, then cover, and simmer for 20 minutes.

Stir the scallions into the chowder with the peas; return to a boil then continue cooking over a medium-heat for a further 5 minutes.

Add the satay sauce or peanut butter to the chowder just before serving. Remove from the heat and stir until melted. Season to taste, then serve, garnished with a spoonful of cream if desired.

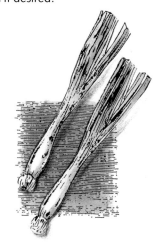

LEMON EGG DROP SOUP

Serves 4

This traditional Greek soup, Avegolemono *has its counterparts in Italy and China. It is essentially simple, but depends on a rich flavorful stock. Fish stock may be used instead of chicken, and rice is often added.*

Ingredients

4 cups chicken stock

2 eggs

3 Tbsp fresh lemon juice, or to taste

Salt and ground black pepper

2 Tbsp chopped fresh parsley

Bring the stock to a boil in a large pan over medium-high heat. Reduce the heat to medium-low so it just simmers.

In a small bowl or measuring cup, beat the eggs and lemon juice with a fork until combined. Season with salt and pepper.

Beat a few tablespoons of the stock into the egg mixture, then very slowly pour the mixture into the soup, whisking slowly and constantly with the fork until the egg is set.

Taste and adjust the seasoning, adding more lemon juice if you wish. Ladle the soup into warm bowls and sprinkle with parsley.

Thai-Spiced Chicken Chowder ▶

DUMPLING SOUP

Serves 6

This Korean dumpling soup contains small dumplings filled with water chestnuts, pork, and chicken, like Chinese dim sum.

Ingredients

1 carrot, chopped

1 onion, chopped

1 garlic clove, chopped

6 water chestnuts, chopped

4 oz lean pork

4 oz chicken

1 cup cooked, shelled shrimp

2 Tbsp soy sauce

1 Tbsp sesame oil

Pinch of Korean chili powder, or cayenne pepper mixed with paprika

30 wonton wrappers

3¾ pt chicken stock (see page 15)

Chopped scallions, to garnish

Put the vegetables and three quarters of the pork, chicken, and shrimp in a food processor. Dice the remaining pork, chicken, and shrimp. Add the soy sauce, sesame oil, and a pinch of Korean chili powder, or cayenne pepper mixed with paprika, to the food processor, and mix to a smooth paste.

Spoon a little of the vegetable mixture into each wonton wrapper. Wet the edges and draw together to make a neat bundle. Pinch the edges together to seal.

Bring the stock to a boil in a pan. Add the dumplings and diced pork, chicken, and shrimp. Simmer for 8 to 10 minutes. Garnish with scallions before serving.

CHICKEN, LEMON, AND MINT SOUP

Serves 4

Traditionally this soup would have been made from an old hen that had ceased to lay. The bird would therefore be tough and require long, gentle poaching to make it tender. It would have been cooked in water but by the end of the cooking time the liquid would be well-flavored and silky-textured. In this modern version, lemon and mint give the soup a clean, fresh taste.

Ingredients

4 chicken pieces
½ Spanish onion, chopped fine
7 cups chicken stock
2 Tbsp short-grain rice
Salt
1½ Tbsp lemon juice
4 Tbsp chopped fine mint

Put the chicken pieces into a heavy flameproof casserole into which they fit comfortably. Add the onion and stock, bring to a simmering point, and remove the scum from the surface. Lower the heat so the liquid barely moves, cover, and cook for 3 minutes. Add the rice and salt, and cook for a further 30 minutes.

Remove the casserole from the heat and leave until the chicken pieces are cool enough to handle. Lift the chicken pieces from the casserole. Discard the skin and remove the meat from the bones. Cut the meat into short strips, return to the casserole, stir in the lemon juice and bring to a boil.

Divide the mint among four soup bowls and ladle in the soup, distributing the chicken flesh and rice evenly.

UDON WITH CURRY SAUCE

Serves 4

A modern Japanese innovation combining the spicy flavor of a curry sauce, with the smooth texture of udon *noodles.*

Ingredients

1¼ lb parboiled fresh *udon*

6 cups *dashi* broth (see page 14)

For the curry

2 Tbsp vegetable oil

2 boneless chicken breasts, diced

1 medium-sized onion, sliced

2 Tbsp flour

1–2 tsp curry powder

½ chicken stock cube

1½ cups water

2 Tbsp chutney

⅓ cup raisins

Salt and ground black pepper

Heat the oil in a pan. Fry the chicken for 5 minutes, or until cooked through. Set aside.

Add the onion, and fry until lightly browned. Add the flour and curry powder, and fry for 1 to 2 minutes.

Gradually dissolve the chicken stock cube into the water, add the chutney and raisins, and season with salt and pepper. Simmer for 10 minutes, then stir in the cooked chicken.

Bring plenty of water to a boil in a pan, and add the *udon*. Cook for 3 minutes, and drain. Rinse under cold water, and drain again. Divide into serving bowls.

Meanwhile, heat the broth. Pour the curry sauce over the *udon*, and pour the broth over the top. Serve immediately.

INDONESIAN CHICKEN SOUP WITH RICE VERMICELLI

Serves 4

Ingredients

2 Tbsp vegetable oil
4 shallots, sliced
3 garlic cloves, sliced
2-inch piece galangal, or 1-inch piece fresh ginger root, sliced
1 tsp ground coriander
3 Tbsp candle or macadamia nuts
3 pt light chicken stock (see page 15)
Cooked chicken meat from the light chicken stock, shredded
2 tsp salt
½ lb rice vermicelli

For the topping

1½ cups bean sprouts, blanched
2 scallions, chopped
1 celery stalk, sliced
2 tsp salt
2 Tbsp ready-made crispy onions
4 lime wedges
2 tsp Indonesian chili paste (*sambal oelek*) or chili sauce

Heat the oil in a frying pan. Fry the shallots, garlic, galangal or ginger, and the coriander, then add the nuts. Blend to a paste with 3 tablespoons chicken stock in a food processor. Put the paste and chicken stock in a pan, and simmer for 5 minutes. Then add the chicken meat and salt, and simmer gently for about 3 minutes. Meanwhile, soak the rice vermicelli in warm water for 3 minutes. Drain, and divide among four bowls.

Put the bean sprouts, scallions, and celery on top of the noodles. Season, pour the soup in, and sprinkle with crispy onions. Garnish with lime wedges and ½ teaspoon of chili sauce to each bowl.

HOT NOODLE SOUP WITH CHICKEN

Serves 4

Ingredients

1 Tbsp vegetable oil
2 garlic cloves, chopped fine
2 shallots, chopped fiine
1-inch piece galangal, or ½-inch piece fresh ginger root, sliced thin
5–6 small red chiles, chopped
4 cups light chicken stock (see page 15)
3 kaffir lime leaves, sliced
2-inch piece lemon grass, sliced
½ lb rice vermicelli

6 Tbsp fish sauce
6 Tbsp fresh lemon juice
2 tsp brown sugar
16 canned straw mushrooms
Chicken meat from the light chicken stock, sliced thin
1 large lettuce leaf, shredded
Cilantro leaves

Heat the oil in a pan; stir-fry the garlic, shallots, galangal or ginger root, and chile for 2 minutes. Add the chicken stock, lime leaves, and lemon grass. Bring to a boil, and simmer gently for 5 minutes.

Soak the rice vermicelli in warm water, rinse, and drain. Divide it among four bowls. Add the fish sauce, lemon juice, sugar, straw mushrooms, and chicken meat to the soup and simmer for 2 to 3 minutes more.

Add the lettuce and cilantro, then simmer for 1 minute. Pour the soup into the bowls, and serve immediately.

CHINESE CHICKEN AND CORN SOUP

Serves 6

This Chinese soup is appreciated around the world. The delicate flavors and subtle spicing make it an approachable and suitably light appetizer for entertaining, not to be reserved just for Asian meals.

Ingredients

3 pt chicken stock

2 boneless skinless chicken breasts

1 small onion, chopped rough

1 carrot, chopped rough

1 celery stalk, chopped rough

1-inch piece fresh ginger root, peeled and sliced

Bouquet garni (parsley stems, leek greens, and bay leaf)

4 ears corn, or 2½ cups thawed frozen or canned corn kernels

8 scallions

Salt and white pepper

3 Tbsp cornstarch, or 4 Tbsp if using kernels (see Cook's tip)

2 egg whites, beaten with 3 Tbsp water

2 oz cooked ham, cut into matchstick strips

Put the stock in a large pan with the chicken, onion, carrot, celery, ginger, and *bouquet garni*. Bring to a boil over medium-high heat, skimming off any foam as it rises to the surface. Reduce the heat to medium-low and simmer, partially covered, for 30 to 40 minutes, or until the chicken is tender. Strain the stock, remove the chicken and discard the vegetables. Shred the chicken.

Cut the kernels from the corn, if using, without cutting down to the cob. With the back of a knife, scrape the cobs to extract the milky liquid from the base of the kernels.

Combine the strained stock, half the scallions, and the corn kernels and their liquid, if available, in the pan, and season with salt and white pepper. Bring to a boil slowly over medium heat and boil gently for 5 minutes.

Stir the cornstarch into 3 tablespoons cold water until dissolved and pour into the soup, stirring constantly. Cook, stirring, until the soup thickens, about 5 minutes. Slowly pour the egg whites into the soup while stirring vigorously. Add the ham and shredded chicken, and heat through, 1 to 2 minutes. Ladle into warm bowls and garnish with the remaining scallions.

Cook's tip

If using frozen or canned corn, it will not thicken the soup as much as the starchy liquid from fresh corn, so increase the cornstarch to 4 tablespoons.

SPICY CHICKEN SOUP

Serves 4

This soup is anything but bland—it has a well-seasoned, true chicken flavor and the vegetables added toward the end have freshness, color, and lots of nutrients. Try adding some of the chicken, shredded or diced, and some noodles for a meal-in-a-dish.

Ingredients

1 onion, halved
2 celery stalks, including leaves, diced
2 carrots, diced
1 parsnip, diced
5 garlic cloves, peeled
3 lb stewing chicken
1½ quarts water
½ tsp fresh basil, minced
½ tsp curry powder
A dash of hot pepper sauce
1 tsp minced cilantro
Salt and ground black pepper

Divide the vegetables in half and place in 2 bowls or on sheets of wax paper. Place the garlic, chicken, and half the vegetables in a Dutch oven or stockpot. Add water to cover the chicken, then the basil, curry powder, hot pepper sauce, cilantro, and salt and pepper to taste. Bring to a boil, then immediately reduce the heat, and simmer uncovered for about 2 hours.

Skim all the fat off the top of the stockpot and strain the soup. Chill the cooked chicken for later use.

Add the remaining vegetables to the soup. Simmer for 10 minutes, or until the vegetables are tender. Serve.

SOBA WITH CHICKEN

Serves 4

The chicken used in this dish should be marinated for as long as you can to extract as much flavor from the sauce as possible, so don't be tempted to cut down on the times below, which should be treated as a minimum.

Ingredients

6 cups *dashi* broth (see page 14)

14 oz dried *soba*

For the topping

3 boneless chicken breasts, sliced on a slant into bite-sized pieces

2 Tbsp Japanese soy sauce

1 leek, sliced thin diagonally

Alfalfa sprouts, to garnish

Thai-7 spice seasoning

Marinate the chicken in the soy sauce for at least 15 minutes. Put the chicken, leek, and *dashi* broth in a saucepan, bring to a boil, and simmer for 10 to 15 minutes, or until the chicken is cooked. Occasionally skim off the scum which will form on top.

Boil plenty of water in a large pan, and add the *soba*. Cook for 5 to 6 minutes. Rinse well under water, and drain thoroughly. Divide the noodles into four bowls.

Pour the broth with chicken and leek into the bowls. Garnish with the sprouts. Sprinkle with the Thai-7 spice, and then serve at once.

TURKEY CHILI SOUP

Serves 6

Chili comes in all colors and this green, relatively mild chili soup has a creamy richness and appealing complexity.

Ingredients

1 Tbsp butter
1 lb skinless boneless turkey, chopped fine or minced
1 onion, chopped fine
2 celery stalks, chopped fine
1 green bell pepper, cored, seeded, and chopped fine
2 garlic cloves, minced
1 green chile pepper, cored, seeded, and chopped fine
4 cups turkey or chicken stock
½ tsp chili powder, or to taste (optional)
4 Tbsp extra virgin olive oil
½ cup blanched almonds
½ cup pitted green olives
Salt and ground black pepper
1 bunch parsley, stalks removed

Melt the butter in a flameproof casserole or large pan over medium heat. Add the turkey and cook, stirring frequently, until lightly browned, about 5 minutes. Stir in the onion, celery, and green bell pepper, and cook until softened. Add the garlic and chile pepper, and continue cooking for 2 to 3 minutes, stirring constantly.

Stir in the stock and bring just to a boil. Reduce the heat to medium-low and simmer for 5 minutes. Taste and add chili powder if you like it hotter.

Meanwhile, put the oil, almonds, olives, and half the parsley in a food processor fitted with a steel blade and process until puréed. Stir the green purée into the soup, season with salt and pepper to taste, and simmer, covered, for 20 minutes.

Finely chop the remaining parsley. Ladle the chili soup into a warm tureen or among bowls and sprinkle with the chopped parsley.

CHICKEN AND VEGETABLE SOUP

Serves 6

Ingredients

3 lb chicken, cut into 8 pieces

6¼ pt chicken stock

4 large tomatoes, peeled, seeded, and chopped; or 2 x 1-lb cans chopped tomatoes, drained

2 medium-sized corn cobs, cut into 3-inch pieces

2 medium yams, peeled and chopped into 1-inch thick slices

2 small potatoes, peeled and cut into 1-inch thick slices

¼ lb pumpkin, peeled and diced

¾ cup fresh or frozen green peas

2 small hot peppers, seeded and sliced thin

2½ tsp salt

Ground black pepper

1½ Tbsp snipped fresh chives

Put the chicken pieces and stock into a large pan, and bring to a boil over high heat. Skim off the foam with a large spoon, then reduce the heat, partially cover, and simmer for 45 minutes.

Skim the fat from the soup. Add the tomatoes, corn, yams, potatoes, pumpkin, peas, hot peppers, salt, and freshly ground black pepper, and bring to a boil. Reduce the heat, and simmer for about 20 minutes or until the chicken and vegetables are cooked.

Taste the soup, adjusting the seasoning if necessary. Stir in the chives, then serve immediately.

TURKEY AND WILD RICE SOUP

Serves 4

Most turkey soups have been devised as a way of using leftover turkey, and this recipe can serve that purpose with a new twist. Try to remember to roast the garlic with the turkey, or put it in the oven to bake with something else. It needs about 30 minutes in a 400°F oven and will keep chilled for 2 to 3 days.

Ingredients

1 head garlic, wrapped in aluminum foil and roasted until soft

3 pt turkey stock

4 oz oyster mushrooms, or other flavorful wild or cultivated mushrooms

1 Tbsp butter

Salt and ground black pepper

1 cup cooked wild rice

1 cup chopped cooked turkey

Oil for frying

12–16 fresh sage leaves, to garnish

Put the garlic and stock in a large pan and bring to a boil slowly over medium heat. Reduce the heat to low and simmer gently, partially covered, for about 20 minutes, or until the garlic has flavored the stock.

Meanwhile, cut the mushrooms into thin strips or slices. Melt the butter in a frying pan over medium heat. Add the mushrooms, season lightly with salt and pepper, and cook, stirring gently and frequently, until lightly browned.

Remove the garlic from the stock with a slotted spoon. Stir in the rice, turkey, and mushrooms and simmer for 10 to 15 minutes.

Pour enough oil into a small pan to cover the bottom generously. Set over high heat until the oil starts to smoke. Add the sage leaves and fry until crispy, about 20 seconds. Drain.

Ladle the soup into a warm tureen or soup bowls and garnish with the sage leaves.

Chicken and Vegetable Soup ▶

BOILED RICE SOUP WITH CHICKEN

Serves 4

The traditional and universal Thai breakfast is tasty and nourishing. It is made with ground pork, and an optional extra is an egg cracked straight into the dish just before serving; it partly poaches in the hot soup.

Ingredients

2¾ pt chicken stock
11 oz boneless skinned chicken breasts, cut across into thin slices
4 cups cooked rice
1 Tbsp chopped pickled cabbage
1 tsp salt
1 tsp ground white pepper
1 cup celery, sliced fine
2 scallions, sliced
⅓ cup garlic cloves, unpeeled and fried until soft
½ cup *phrik dong* (sliced red chile with vinegar)
2 Tbsp fish sauce

Boil the chicken stock in a pan. Add the chicken, rice, cabbage, salt, and pepper; boil the chicken until cooked, about 8 to 10 minutes. Add the celery and scallion, and then remove from the heat immediately.

Pour into bowls and sprinkle with the fried garlic. Serve with the *phrik dong* and fish sauce in separate bowls.

GAME BIRD CONSOMME WITH POACHED QUAIL EGGS

Serves 4

This is not a classic consommé, as it is not clarified. Cooking it slowly is an easy and effective method to achieve a relatively clear stock and retain the delicate flavor that would be lost in the clarification process.

Ingredients

1 large game bird carcass, such as pheasant or duck, or 3–4 small ones, such as pigeon or quail, raw or cooked and trimmed of excess fat

1 large onion, quartered

2 carrots, chopped coarse

1 parsnip, chopped coarse

1 leek, sliced

2–4 garlic cloves, crushed

1 Tbsp black peppercorns

Bouquet garni (thyme sprigs, parsley stems, tarragon or sage leaves, and bay leaf)

3 cups cold chicken stock

Salt (optional)

2–3 Tbsp dry sherry

8 quail eggs

Fresh chervil or Italian parsley, to garnish

Put the carcass(es), onion, carrots, parsnip, leek, garlic, peppercorns, and *bouquet garni* in a stockpot or large heavy pan. Add the stock and enough cold water to cover the ingredients by 1 inch. Bring slowly to a boil over medium heat, skimming the foam that rises to the surface often. Reduce the heat to low and simmer for 1½ to 2 hours. Strain the stock through a strainer lined with damp cheesecloth into a bowl and if any meat can be picked off the carcass(es), reserve it. Cool the stock and chill for several hours or overnight. Skim off any congealed fat and blot the surface with a paper towel to remove any remaining fat.

Bring a small pan of salted water to a boil and poach the quail eggs, a few at a time, for 2 to 3 minutes, or until done as you like them. Remove with a slotted spoon to a bowl of tepid water to stop further cooking. Trim off any untidy bits of white.

Bring the stock just to a boil and reduce the heat to medium-low. Taste and season with a little salt, if needed, and stir in the sherry. If the stock is bland, reduce it slightly with a fresh *bouquet garni*.

Place the poached eggs in warm shallow soup plates, ladle over the consommé, and garnish with chervil or parsley leaves.

PHEASANT SOUP WITH LIVER DUMPLINGS

Serves 4

This soup is great for gourmet hunters! Make it after roasting pheasant, using leftover cooked meat and stock made from the carcasses, or make stock from the remaining parts of raw birds after the breasts have been removed for serving separately.

Ingredients

3 pt pheasant stock

2 cups cubed cooked pheasant

1 Tbsp chopped fresh parsley

1 Tbsp snipped fresh chives and/or tarragon

For the liver dumplings

1 Tbsp butter, plus more for frying

1 shallot, chopped fine

2 garlic cloves, minced

⅓ cup pheasant or chicken livers

1 egg, beaten

1 Tbsp heavy cream

1 cup fresh white bread crumbs

1 tsp chopped fresh thyme

Salt and ground black pepper

Combine the stock and pheasant meat in a large pan, together with the herbs. Bring to a boil, reduce the heat to low, and simmer for about 15 minutes.

For the liver dumplings, melt half the butter in a small shallow frying pan over medium-low heat and cook the shallots and garlic for 3 to 4 minutes until softened. Remove to cool. Add the remaining butter, increase the heat to medium-high, and cook the livers for 2 to 3 minutes until browned, turning to color evenly. Remove and leave to cool slightly.

Beat together the egg and cream in a small bowl. Add the bread crumbs, stir to combine, and allow to stand until the bread has absorbed the egg, 1 to 2 minutes. Put the livers in a food processor fitted with a steel blade and pulse to chop fine. Add the thyme, seasoning, shallots, garlic, and soaked bread, and then process to mix well.

To cook the dumplings, melt a little butter in a frying pan over medium heat. Shape the mixture into small balls about the size of chestnuts. Flatten them slightly and fry gently until lightly browned, about 3 minutes, turning once. Drain on paper towels.

Divide the dumplings among warm soup bowls. Ladle over the hot soup and sprinkle with herbs.

CHICKEN AND CHILE SOUP

Serves 4–6

Ingredients

1 tsp oil
1 tsp green curry paste
2½ cups chicken stock
⅔ cup coconut milk
1 or 2 bird's eye (Thai) chiles, seeded and chopped
2 lemon grass stalks, outer leaves removed and chopped fine
4 kaffir lime leaves
1-inch piece ginger root, peeled and shredded
12 oz chicken breasts, skinned and cut into thin strips
1 cup green beans, trimmed and cut into short pieces
3-inch piece cucumber, peeled if preferred and cut into strips
½ cup cooked fragrant rice
1–2 tsp honey
4 Tbsp light cream (optional)

Heat the oil in a large pan and fry the curry paste gently for 3 minutes, stirring occasionally.

Add the stock with the coconut milk, chiles, lemon grass, lime leaves, and ginger. Bring to a boil and boil for 3 minutes. Reduce the heat, then add the chicken strips, and simmer gently for 5 to 10 minutes, or until the chicken is cooked.

Add the green beans and cucumber with the rice and honey. Simmer for a further 5 minutes.

Stir in the cream, if using, and serve.

CHICKEN SOUP WITH HOMEMADE NOODLES

Serves 6

These golden egg noodles are worth the effort, but if time is short, save noodle-making for another day, or simmer good quality bought fresh pasta in the soup.

Ingredients

4 chicken leg quarters, about 1¾ lb, skinned
4 pt chicken stock
1 celery stalk, chopped rough
1 carrot, chopped rough
1 onion, sliced
1 garlic clove, crushed
5 peppercorns
Large *bouquet garni* (parsley, thyme sprigs, and bay leaf)
1 Tbsp butter
5 oz mushrooms, sliced
2 Tbsp chopped fresh parsley

For the noodles

1 cup flour
¼ tsp salt
2 egg yolks
1 tsp extra virgin olive oil
A pinch saffron threads, soaked in 2 Tbsp hot water

For the noodles, put the flour and salt into a food processor and pulse to combine. In a small bowl, beat together the egg yolks and oil, strain in the saffron liquid, and beat to mix; discard the threads. With the machine running, pour in the egg yolk mixture and continue running until it forms a ball which leaves the bowl virtually clean. If this doesn't happen and the dough seems a bit sticky, add 2 tablespoons of flour and continue kneading in the food processor until the dough does not stick to your hands. Wrap and chill for 30 minutes.

Divide the dough into quarters and roll out on a floured surface to less than ¹⁄₁₆ inch, and cut into diamond shapes about 1½ inches on each side. Let the noodles dry in a single layer on floured wire racks or baking sheets for 1 hour.

Put the chicken in a large pan with the stock, celery, carrot, onion, garlic, peppercorns, and *bouquet garni*. Bring just to a boil over medium-high heat, skimming off the foam. Reduce the heat to medium-low and simmer, partially covered, for about 45 minutes, skimming as needed.

Remove the chicken from the stock and set aside to cool. Continue simmering the stock, uncovered, for about 30 minutes. When the chicken is cool, take the meat from the bones and cut into bite-sized pieces. Strain the stock and remove the fat; discard the *bouquet garni* and vegetables.

Melt the butter in a large pan or flameproof casserole over medium heat. Add the mushrooms and 1 tablespoon of water and cook until browned, stirring frequently. Add the stock and bring to a boil. Stir in the noodles and boil for 10 minutes. Return the chicken to the stock and continue cooking for 5 to 10 minutes longer. Ladle the soup into warm shallow bowls and sprinkle with parsley.

CURRIED CHICKEN CHOWDER

Serves 4

The subtle curry and slightly tart apple flavors give this soup a pleasing complexity that makes it suitable for the most elegant occasions. The strength of curry powders varies, so use your own judgment, but it should not dominate.

Ingredients

2 Tbsp butter
1 onion, chopped fine
1 garlic clove, minced
3 Tbsp flour
1 tsp curry powder
2 small carrots, halved lengthwise and sliced thin
1 celery stalk, sliced thin
1 potato, diced
4 cups chicken stock
Bouquet garni (parsley, thyme sprigs, and bay leaf)
Salt and ground black pepper
1 dessert apple, peeled, cored, and diced
2 cups cubed cooked chicken
4–6 Tbsp heavy cream
2 Tbsp snipped fresh chives, to garnish

Melt the butter in a large, heavy pan over medium heat. Add the onion and garlic. Cook, stirring frequently, until the vegetables start to soften, about 5 minutes. Stir in the flour and curry powder and cook for 2 minutes. Stir in the carrots, celery, potato, and stock. Bring to a boil, stirring frequently. Add the *bouquet garni* and season with salt and pepper.

Reduce the heat to medium-low and simmer, stirring occasionally, until the vegetables are almost tender, about 20 minutes. Add the apple and chicken, and continue cooking for about 10 minutes, or until the apple is tender. Remove the *bouquet garni*.

Stir in the cream, taste and adjust the seasoning, and heat through. Ladle into warm bowls and garnish with chives.

Meat Soups

SAUSAGE AND TOMATO SOUP

Serves 6

This hearty, warming soup is filling enough for a main course. Use good-quality sausages from a reputable delicatessen to be sure of the best results.

Ingredients

2 slices bacon, chopped
8 oz garlic-flavored smoked sausage
8 oz morcela sausage or blood sausage
1 Spanish onion, halved and sliced
2 garlic cloves, crushed
$2\frac{1}{4}$ lb well-flavored tomatoes, chopped
1 bay leaf
$4\frac{1}{4}$ cups vegetable or chicken stock or water
Salt and ground black pepper
Firm country bread, to serve

Cook the bacon gently in a heavy pan until the fat has been rendered.

Prick the sausages and cook with the bacon for a few minutes, stirring two or three times, before stirring in the onion and garlic. Cook until softened; then add the tomatoes, bay leaf, and stock or water.

Bring to a boil and simmer gently, uncovered, for about 30 minutes.

Remove the sausages and slice, return to the pan, reheat, and season. Serve with firm country bread.

SAUSAGE, APPLE, AND PASTA SOUP

Serves 4

This is definitely a main course soup! If you don't eat meat, serve cubed cheese, which will start to melt in the soup. Standard pork sausages have been used, but a spicier variety could be used.

Ingredients

2 Tbsp vegetable oil
1 lb pork sausages
1 onion, chopped fine
1 red bell pepper, seeded and chopped
$\frac{1}{2}$ cup dry cider
3 cups stock
Salt and ground black pepper
$\frac{1}{2}$ tsp grated nutmeg
$3\frac{1}{2}$ oz whole-wheat macaroni
1 large cooking apple, chopped fine
$\frac{1}{2}$ cup shredded Cheddar cheese (optional)

Heat the oil in a large pan, then add the sausages, and cook quickly until browned on all sides. Add the onion and bell pepper and cook more slowly for 3 to 4 minutes, until the vegetables are soft.

Add the cider and stock to the pan with the seasonings and bring to a boil. Simmer the soup for 30 minutes, then remove the sausages with a slotted spoon. Add the macaroni and simmer for a further 10 to 12 minutes, or until the pasta is cooked. Slice the sausages while the macaroni is cooking and then return the meat to the pan. Add the apple just before the pasta is cooked – do not simmer it for more than 2 minutes.

Season the soup to taste then serve immediately, with or without shredded cheese.

Sausage and Tomato Soup ▶

LAMB AND VEGETABLE SOUP WITH VERMICELLI

Serves 6

Variations of this thickened vermicelli soup can be found throughout North Africa. The lamb is simmered to become tender and succulent.

Ingredients

3 Tbsp olive oil
4 onions, chopped
3 cloves garlic, crushed
3 red bell peppers, chopped
1½ lb lean lamb, cubed
2 lamb bones, cracked
4 pt meat stock or water
Salt and ground black pepper
A pinch of crushed dried red chiles
4 tomatoes, chopped
½ cup dried apricots
1–1½ Tbsp chopped fresh mint
½ cup vermicelli
1 Tbsp lemon juice
Chopped fresh parsley and mint, to garnish

Heat the oil in a large pan, then cook the onions, garlic, bell peppers, and lamb, stirring occasionally, for 10 minutes. Add the bones, stock, seasoning, chile, tomatoes, apricots, and mint and bring just to a boil then simmer for about 1¼ to 1½ hours until the lamb is very tender.

Bring to a boil, add the vermicelli and cook for 5 minutes until tender. Pour the soup into a warmed tureen, stir in the lemon juice and garnish with chopped parsley and mint.

ISSAAN-STYLE SOUP

Serves 4–6

Ingredients

4 oz each beef or calf's heart, liver, kidney (any offal may be used, depending on your preference), cleaned and prepared
5 cups water
1 oz galangal, sliced
3 stalks lemon grass, cut into 1¼-inch pieces and crushed
5 kaffir lime leaves, shredded
1½ Tbsp fish sauce
1 Tbsp lemon juice
2 dried red chiles, crushed
½ tsp salt
1 scallion, cut into ½-inch pieces

Boil all the offal together in a pan of water until tender, about 30 to 40 minutes. Rinse well in cold water and slice up fairly small.

Place the cooked offal in a pan with the water, bring to a boil, and add all the remaining ingredients except the scallion. Bring back to a boil for 2 minutes, add the scallion, and remove from the heat.

Serve immediately, accompanied by sticky or steamed rice, if you like.

Lamb and Vegetable Soup with Vermicelli ▶

BEEF, EGGPLANT, AND BELL PEPPER SOUP

Serves 4–6

A spicy broth or soup with the flavors of the Pacific Rim. Serve this as a lunch or supper dish with bread, or you could add a spoonful of cooked rice to each helping to make it more substantial.

Ingredients

¼ lb boneless chuck steak

3 Tbsp peanut oil

1 large onion, chopped fine

1 small eggplant, cut into ¼-inch dice

1 hot red chile, seeded and chopped fine

1 green bell pepper, cored, seeded, and chopped

1-inch piece fresh ginger root, peeled and sliced fine

1 stick lemon grass, bruised and chopped fine

3 fresh lime leaves, shredded fine (use dried if fresh are unavailable)

5 cups well-flavored broth

Soy sauce and salt, to taste

Cut the beef into ½-inch strips, then slice it very fine. Heat the oil in a large pan, add the beef and cook quickly until well browned. Add the onion, eggplant, chile, bell pepper, ginger, and lemon grass, then cover the pan and cook slowly for 4 to 5 minutes.

Add the lime leaves and broth, then bring to a boil. Cover and simmer for at least 1 hour, until all the ingredients are tender and the flavors have blended.

Season to taste with soy sauce and salt before serving.

"ALMOST NOTHING" SOUP

Serves 4–6

This Russian soup made from scraps, has a surprising flavor, smoky and nut-like. Add a little cream, to make it more sophisticated.

Ingredients

3 lb beef, chicken, veal, or mixed bones
1 onion, unpeeled
Salt and ground black pepper
4¼ pt water
2 lb potatoes, scrubbed and dried
½ cup bacon fat or melted butter
1 large onion, peeled and chopped
½ cup light cream (optional)
2 Tbsp snipped fresh chives

Place the bones, the unpeeled onion, and seasoning to taste in a large pan. Cover with the water, and put over high heat. Bring to a boil, then cover, and simmer for 1 hour. Uncover and continue to simmer until the stock has reduced by almost half. Strain the stock and return to the saucepan.

Meanwhile peel the potatoes. Reserve the potatoes themselves for another use. Melt the bacon fat or butter in a frying pan and sauté the onion until soft, about 6 minutes. Add the potato skins and continue to cook until they are tender.

Transfer the potato skins and onion to the pot containing the stock. Bring to a boil, then reduce the heat and simmer for 10 minutes. Purée the soup in batches; return to the pot and reheat. Thin, if necessary, with a little water or the cream. Ladle into individual bowls and serve immediately sprinkled with the chopped chives.

GEORGIAN SPICY BEEF SOUP WITH PLUMS

Serves 6

This slightly sour soup appears in many versions. It is often flavored with dried plums, but fresh plums add the necessary tartness and are easier to find. Fenugreek is an essential ingredient for authenticity, but its unusual taste is not pleasing to everyone and it can be difficult to obtain. Do not hesitate to try the soup with or without it.

Ingredients

4 garlic cloves
5 allspice berries
10 peppercorns
15 coriander seeds
½ tsp fenugreek seeds
½ tsp crushed red pepper flakes
2 lb boneless stewing beef, cut in 1-inch cubes
2 onions, chopped fine
1 carrot, chopped fine
Large *bouquet garni* (2 bay leaves, cilantro and parsley, thyme and savory sprigs, and celery leaves)
5 pt water
2 tsp vegetable oil
2 garlic cloves, minced
6 tomatoes, preferably plum, peeled, seeded, and chopped
6 large plums, pitted, peeled, and chopped fine
½ tsp dried summer savory
½ tsp dried fenugreek leaves, crushed
¼ tsp turmeric
¼ tsp hot paprika, or a pinch of cayenne pepper
Salt
Lemon juice, to taste
1–2 Tbsp plum preserves (optional)
3 Tbsp chopped cilantro, to garnish

Lightly crush 2 of the garlic cloves and put them in a piece of cheesecloth with the allspice berries, peppercorns, coriander and fenugreek seeds, and red pepper flakes. Tie with string.

Put the cubes of beef in a flameproof casserole or large pan with half the onions and the carrot. Add the *bouquet garni* spice bag and water. Bring to a boil over medium-high heat, skimming off any foam as it rises to the surface. Reduce the heat to low and simmer, partially covered, for 1½ to 2 hours until the meat is very tender, skimming as necessary and stirring occasionally.

Strain the cooking liquid and discard the vegetables, and *bouquet garni* spice bag. Spoon off the fat from the cooking liquid. (If preparing the recipe in advance, chill the meat until needed. Cool the cooking liquid and chill, covered; remove the fat when it is congealed and hard.)

Heat the oil in a large pan, add the remaining onions, and cook over medium heat until just softened, about 3 minutes. Add the garlic, tomatoes, plums, savory, dried fenugreek, turmeric, paprika or cayenne, and a little salt, and continue cooking for 5 minutes, stirring frequently. Add the beef and its cooking liquid, bring to a boil, reduce the heat to low, and simmer for about 45 minutes, stirring occasionally.

Taste and adjust the seasoning and stir in a few drops of lemon juice, or as needed, and if you wish, the plum preserves. (The soup should be slightly sour.) Ladle into warm bowls and sprinkle with the cilantro.

Georgian Spicy Beef Soup with Plums ▶

RABBIT AND LEEK SOUP WITH PRUNES

Serves 6

Rabbit is traditionally paired with prunes. If you are able to obtain a wild rabbit, the flavor of the soup will be more robust.

Ingredients

3 large leeks
1 Tbsp vegetable oil
2 lb rabbit pieces
6 Tbsp dry white wine
2 cups water
3 garlic cloves, crushed
4–5 fresh thyme sprigs or ½ tsp dried thyme
1 bay leaf
3 pt chicken stock
18 pitted prunes, about 6 oz
Salt and ground black pepper

Thinly slice the white part of the leeks and reserve. Chop up the green parts of the leeks.

Heat the oil in a large flameproof casserole over medium-high heat. Add the rabbit pieces and cook until golden brown, turning to color evenly. Add the wine and water, bring to a boil, and add the chopped green part of the leeks, garlic, and herbs. Add the stock, reduce the heat to low, cover, and simmer very gently for about 1 hour until the rabbit is tender. (Wild rabbit may take longer.) Strain the cooking liquid and discard the vegetables and herbs. When cool enough to handle, take the rabbit meat from the bones.

Remove as much fat as possible from the cooking liquid and put it in a large pan with the rabbit meat, sliced leeks, and prunes. Season with salt and pepper to taste. Bring to a boil over medium-high heat, reduce the heat to low, and simmer gently, stirring occasionally, until the leeks are tender. Taste and adjust the seasoning, if needed, and ladle the soup into a warm tureen or among warmed serving bowls.

MEATBALL SOUP WITH CABBAGE AND PARMESAN CHEESE

Serves 8

These flavorful meatballs can be shaped and browned ahead, so the final preparation of the soup is easier.
Make them quite small so they are really bite-sized.

Ingredients

1 large onion, halved
4–5 Tbsp olive oil
1 garlic clove, minced fine
1 cup soft bread crumbs
1 lb lean ground beef or veal
1 egg, lightly beaten
¾ tsp chopped fresh thyme, or ¼ tsp dried
¾ tsp chopped fresh marjoram leaves, or ¼ tsp dried
2 Tbsp shredded Parmesan cheese, plus more for serving
Salt and ground black pepper
Flour for coating
12 oz young green cabbage, cored, quartered, and sliced thin
1½ lb tomatoes, peeled, seeded, and chopped
4 cups brown chicken or beef stock

Chop half the onion finely. Slice the other half thinly and reserve. Heat 2 teaspoons of the oil in a small frying pan over medium heat and cook the chopped onion until just softened, about 3 minutes, stirring frequently. Add the garlic and continue cooking for 2 minutes longer. Then remove from the heat and allow to cool slightly.

Put the bread crumbs in a small bowl and cover with water. Let stand for 2 minutes, drain and squeeze dry. In a mixing bowl, combine the bread crumbs, chopped onion, meat, egg, thyme, marjoram, and Parmesan cheese. Season with salt, if needed, and plenty of pepper. Mix thoroughly and roll into small balls about ¾ inch in diameter. Roll the balls in flour to coat lightly.

Heat 2 tablespoons of the remaining oil in a large frying pan over medium-high heat. Brown the meatballs in batches, not crowding the pan and turning to color evenly. Remove and drain on paper towels. (Chill, if making in advance.)

Heat the remaining oil in a large pan over medium heat. Add the reserved onion slices and cabbage, and cook for 3 to 4 minutes, stirring frequently, until they start to wilt. Add the tomatoes, stock, and meatballs. Bring to a boil, reduce the heat to medium-low and simmer for about 20 minutes, or until the vegetables are tender. Taste and adjust the seasoning if necessary. Ladle into warm bowls and serve sprinkled with Parmesan cheese.

RAMEN WITH BARBECUED PORK

Serves 4

Cha siu *is a spicy Chinese marinade, and* cha siu *pork is widely eaten all over southeast Asia. This meaty soup is ideal for a hearty main course.* Cha siu *sauce is available from Chinese stores and larger supermarkets.*

Ingredients

1 lb *ramen* noodles, or 14 oz fresh or ¾ lb dried thin egg noodles

3 pt soy sauce broth (see page 15)

For the topping

12 large slices Chinese-style barbecued pork (*cha siu*)

4 Tbsp cooked dried bamboo shoots (*shinachiku*) (optional)

3 scallions, chopped

Boil plenty of water in a pan, and cook the noodles for 3 minutes. Drain and divide into four bowls. Heat the soy sauce broth.

Put three slices of *cha siu* into each bowl of noodles. Garnish with the bamboo shoots and scallions. Pour the soy sauce broth over the top just before serving hot.

BEEF AND SEAWEED SOUP

Serves 6

Wrap the meat and put it in the freezer for about 35 minutes to make cutting it into strips easier. Wakame is the Japanese name for a green type of seaweed available dried in packages from Asian specialty stores.

Ingredients

4 oz dried *wakame*, soaked for at least 30 minutes

3 pt fish or beef stock

1 bunch scallions, white and some green parts chopped

1 Tbsp sesame oil

1 garlic clove, crushed

6 oz lean tender beef, cut into fine strips

Soy sauce

Toasted sesame seeds, to garnish

Drain the *wakame* and cut it into fine strips.

Pour the stock into a pan. Add the scallions and bring to a boil. Lower the heat so the stock simmers slowly. Heat the oil in a frying pan. Add the garlic and beef and stir-fry for about 2 minutes. Add to the stock together with the *wakame*. Add soy sauce to taste and heat through. Serve garnished with toasted sesame seeds.

PEA AND HAM SOUP

Serves 4

Ingredients

2 large onions

2 Tbsp bacon fat

1 ham bone and trimmings or 2 knuckles of bacon

1 lb dried peas (soaked for at least 3 hours)

1 bunch of fresh herbs

1 bay leaf

4–5 pt bacon stock or water used for boiling ham

Salt and ground black pepper

Chopped fresh mint and parsley

Soften the onions in the bacon fat. Put them in a large pan with the ham bone or knuckles and add the soaked peas, the bunch of herbs, and bay leaf. Cover these with the stock or ham water. Bring the stock slowly to a boil, then simmer for 2 hours.

Take out the bones—dice any ham or bacon trimmings, which can go back into the soup.

If the soup is too thick, water or milk may be added to thin it. If you add milk, bring the soup to simmering point, but do not boil it.

Season and serve with chopped mint and parsley. Small pieces of bacon are a nice addition.

Cook's tip

Dried whole peas, marrow fats, or split green peas may be used for this soup. Yellow peas may also be used and taste just as good, but the green color is more appealing with the ham.

ITALIAN SAUSAGE AND ZUCCHINI SOUP

Serves 4–6

This soup emphasizes the fennel used to flavor many Italian sausages. If other sausages are used, add a pinch of fennel seeds to the soup. The lemon, garlic, and parsley seasoning, or gremolata, a traditional Italian garnish for stews and seafood, brings a pleasant zing to the soup.

Ingredients

1 lb sweet Italian sausages

1 Tbsp olive oil

1 large onion, chopped fine

2 garlic cloves, minced

1 fennel bulb, chopped fine

½ red or yellow bell pepper, seeded and chopped fine

1 lb zucchini, shredded

3 pt brown chicken or beef stock

1 tsp chopped fresh marjoram or ¼ tsp dried

1 tsp chopped fresh thyme or ¼ tsp dried

1 bay leaf

Salt and ground black pepper

For the lemon-garlic seasoning

Grated rind of ½ lemon (unwaxed or scrubbed)

1 garlic clove, minced

2 Tbsp chopped fresh parsley

Put the sausages in a frying pan and set over medium heat. Cook until well browned, turning to color evenly. Remove and drain on paper towels. Cut into slices.

Heat the oil in a heavy pan or flameproof casserole over medium-high heat. Add the onion, garlic, fennel, and pepper, and cook for 3 to 4 minutes, stirring occasionally, until slightly softened.

Add the zucchini, stock, and herbs. Stir in the sliced sausages, reduce the heat to low, and simmer for about 20 minutes. Add a little stock or water if you like a thinner soup. Season to taste with salt, if needed, and pepper. Discard the bay leaf.

For the lemon-garlic seasoning, chop together the lemon rind, garlic, and parsley until very fine and stir into the soup. Heat through and ladle into a warm tureen or bowls.

ARAB LAMB AND GARBANZO SOUP

Serves 4–6

Redolent of exotic Middle Eastern spices, this soup, a slightly tamed version of the Moroccan mutton soup Harira, is satisfying and unusual. Lentils, dried beans, or pasta are sometimes added for an even more substantial soup and in Morocco, dates are offered as an accompaniment.

Ingredients

¾ cup garbanzo beans, soaked overnight and drained, or 1¾ cups canned chickpeas, rinsed and drained

1½–2 Tbsp olive oil

1½ lb boneless lamb shoulder, trimmed of all fat and cut into 1-inch cubes

1 onion, chopped fine

3 garlic cloves, minced

4 Tbsp dry white wine (optional)

5 cups water

¾ tsp dried thyme

¾ tsp dried oregano

1 bay leaf

¼ tsp ground cinnamon

¼ tsp cumin seeds

4 tomatoes, peeled, seeded, and chopped, or 1 cup tomato juice

2 roasted red bell peppers, peeled, seeded, and chopped

¼ tsp ground saffron or turmeric

1 large leek, halved lengthwise and sliced

1 large carrot, diced

1 large potato, diced

2 medium zucchini, halved lengthwise and sliced

⅔ cup fresh or thawed frozen green peas

Harissa (hot red pepper paste, see page 126), to taste

Chopped fresh mint, or cilantro, to garnish

If using dried garbanzos, cook over medium heat in boiling unsalted water to cover generously until tender, about 1½ hours. Drain.

Heat the oil in a flameproof casserole or large heavy pan over high heat. Add enough of the lamb to cover the base of the pan sparsely and cook, stirring frequently, until evenly browned. Remove the browned meat and continue cooking in batches, adding a little more oil if needed. When the last batch is nearly browned, add the onion and garlic, and cook, stirring frequently, for 2 minutes. Return all the meat to the pan and add the wine, if using, water, thyme, oregano, bay leaf, cinnamon, and cumin. Bring just to a boil, skimming off any foam as it rises to the surface, reduce the heat to low and simmer for about 1½ hours until the meat is very tender. Discard the bay leaf.

Stir in the garbanzos, tomatoes or tomato juice, roasted bell peppers, saffron or turmeric, leek, carrot, and potato, and simmer for 15 minutes. Add the zucchini and beans, and continue simmering for 15 to 20 minutes more, or until all the vegetables are tender. Taste and adjust the seasoning, adding a little *Harissa*, if you like a spicier soup.

Ladle the soup into a warmed tureen or bowls and sprinkle with fresh mint or cilantro.

Arab Lamb and Chickpea Soup ▶

FRUIT SOUPS

SUNSET FRUIT SOUP

Serves 6–8

Intensely colored exotic fruit purées arranged in adjoining bands make a dramatic presentation. Shallow glass soup plates or other very shallow plain dishes are most effective for serving this soup.

Ingredients

¼ cup sugar
¼ cup water
1 small pineapple, peeled and cored
½ cup lime juice
1 large mango
1 large papaya

Combine the sugar and water in a small pan and bring to a boil, stirring occasionally. Remove from the heat and let the syrup cool.

Cut the pineapple into chunks and put in a food processor fitted with a steel blade with 1 tablespoon of the lime juice and 3 tablespoons of the sugar syrup. Purée until smooth. Scrape into a small bowl, cover, and chill.

Peel the mango. Cut down each side of the center stone and put the flesh in the food processor (no need to wash it between puréeing each fruit), then cut off all the flesh adhering to the stone and add it to the bowl. Add 3 tablespoons of the lime juice and 2 tablespoons of the sugar syrup and purée until smooth. Scrape into a small bowl, cover, and chill.

Halve the papaya and discard the seeds. Scoop the flesh into the food processor, leaving almost none remaining on the skin. Add the remaining lime juice and sugar syrup and purée until smooth. Scrape into a small bowl, cover, and chill.

To serve, arrange the fruit purées in chilled shallow bowls or dishes in adjoining bands from lightest to darkest colors.

Cook's tip

If any one of the fruits is unavailable, substitute yellow- or orange-fleshed melon.

STRAWBERRY SOUP

Serves 6

At the height of the strawberry season, celebrate their perfection with this soup. If your berries are honey-sweet, you may not need any sugar!

Ingredients

1½ lb strawberries, hulled
Juice of 1 lemon
4 Tbsp sugar, or to taste
2 cups freshly squeezed, strained orange juice
3 Tbsp Cointreau or Kirsch
½ cup heavy cream
Mint sprigs or strawberry leaves, to decorate

Reserve 6 berries to decorate and put the remainder in a food processor fitted with a steel blade or in a blender. Add the lemon juice and sugar, depending on the sweetness of the berries and your taste, and purée.

Strain the purée into a bowl and stir in the orange juice and Cointreau or Kirsch. Cover and chill until cold.

Whip the cream until it forms soft peaks. Ladle the soup into chilled shallow bowls, preferably glass, and top each serving with a dollop of whipped cream. Decorate with the reserved berries and mint sprigs or strawberry leaves.

Sunset Fruit Soup ▶

CHILLED MELON-SANGRIA SOUP

Serves 6

Chilled fruit soup, made with melons from California's Imperial or San Joaquin Valley, is a delightful start to a summer meal. Use honeydew, cantaloupe, Crenshaw, Persian or casaba melons. The soup highlights the flavor of the melon, so be sure to pick ripe melons. You can substitute lemonade or soda water or more orange juice for the wine.

Ingredients

About 1 large or 2 small cantaloupe melons, cubed

½ cup sweet white wine, such as Riesling or Gewürztraminer

½ cup orange juice

2 Tbsp fresh lime juice

½ tsp grated nutmeg

1 Tbsp honey (optional)

Strawberries, to garnish

Place all the ingredients except for the honey and strawberries in a blender or food processor. Process until the melon is puréed and ingredients are well mixed.

Taste and add honey if needed. Chill. Serve cold, garnished with strawberries.

MINTED MELON SOUP

Serves 4

Only ripe melons will do for this cold soup, in fact the melon purée can be made from slightly overripe melons. Use whatever varieties are available, as long as they are different colors. Serve this soup either as an appetizer or dessert.

Ingredients

1 large ripe green-fleshed melon, such as honeydew, Galia or Ogen

5–6 mint leaves, plus more to decorate

⅔ cup medium Muscat wine

½ cup water

1–2 Tbsp lime juice (optional)

2–3 Tbsp superfine sugar

½ large ripe orange-fleshed melon, such as cantaloupe, Charentais, or casaba

Discard the seeds from the green-fleshed melon and scoop the flesh into a blender or a food processor fitted with a steel blade. Add the mint, wine, water, lime juice, if using, and sugar. Purée until smooth and then chill, covered.

Discard the seeds of the orange-fleshed melon and, using a melon baller, scoop out the flesh in small balls, or cut into cubes. Cover and chill.

To serve, divide the melon purée among four chilled bowls. Arrange the melon balls on top, dividing them evenly, and decorate with mint.

CITRUS SOUP

Serves 4

The richness of the smooth custard is a perfect background for the pleasantly sharp citrus fruit.

Ingredients

1 vanilla bean

1¼ cups whole milk

1 egg

2 egg yolks

5 Tbsp sugar

1 Tbsp Cointreau or other orange liqueur

2 large seedless oranges (unwaxed)

1 ruby grapefruit

Put the vanilla bean and milk in a medium pan and bring just to a boil over medium-high heat, stirring frequently. Remove from the heat and cover. Allow to stand for 15 to 20 minutes and remove the vanilla bean.

In a medium bowl, whisk the egg, egg yolks, and 2 tablespoons of the sugar for 2 to 3 minutes until thick and creamy. Whisk in the hot milk and return the mixture to the pan. With a wooden spoon, stir over medium-low heat until the custard thickens and coats the back of the spoon (do not allow it to boil or the custard may curdle). Immediately strain into a cold bowl set in a larger bowl of ice water and allow to cool, stirring occasionally. Stir in the Cointreau and chill, covered.

With a vegetable peeler, remove the rind from one of the oranges in wide strips. Stack two or three strips at a time and slice into thin slivers. Combine the remaining sugar and 5 tablespoons of water in a small pan and bring to a boil, stirring occasionally. Add the orange zest, reduce the heat, and simmer for 10 minutes. Remove from the heat and allow to cool.

Peel the oranges and grapefruit, working over a bowl to catch the juices, and segment the fruit by cutting between the membranes. Add 3 to 4 tablespoons of the juice to the custard.

Divide the custard among four chilled shallow bowls. Arrange the fruit in a starburst pattern on top and decorate with orange zest.

ICED PASSION FRUIT SOUP WITH YOGURT AND VANILLA

Serves 4

Look for passion fruits that are large and heavy with dimpled skin. They can be expensive so you'll probably want to reserve this recipe for a special occasion.

Ingredients

20 fresh passion fruits
½ cup sugar
4-inch piece of vanilla bean, split lengthwise
1 cup water
2 tsp unflavored gelatin
½ cup plain yogurt, whisked well
Fresh mint leaves, to decorate (optional)

Place a coarse strainer over a medium nonreactive pan. Working over the strainer, cut each passion fruit in half, and then scoop out the pulp with a teaspoon. Push the pulp and juice through the strainer, and discard the seeds.

Add the sugar, vanilla bean, and water to the pan and bring to a simmer over low heat, stirring. Remove from the heat and sprinkle the gelatin evenly over the mixture. Set aside, undisturbed, to let the gelatin thicken on the surface of the juice, about 3 minutes. Then whisk the mixture well to incorporate the gelatin. Set a fine strainer over a medium nonreactive bowl and strain the mixture. Leave to cool to room temperature, then place the bowl in a larger bowl filled with ice and water. Chill the mixture over the ice, stirring frequently. (The recipe can be prepared to this point and then chilled overnight.)

To serve, ladle the chilled soup into four shallow soup dishes. Top each serving with 2 tablespoons yogurt and top with mint leaves if desired.

BREADFRUIT SOUP

Serves 6

Ingredients

4 Tbsp butter or margarine
1 medium onion, chopped fine
1 garlic clove, minced
6 oz fresh breadfruit, peeled, cored, and chopped
2½ cups chicken stock
1¼ cups light cream
1 tsp salt
¼ tsp ground black pepper
2 tsp chopped fresh parsley

Melt the butter or margarine in a large pan. Add the onion and garlic and cook for 5 minutes, stirring until they are soft. Add the breadfruit and chicken stock and bring to a boil. Reduce the heat and simmer for 20 minutes, or until the breadfruit is tender.

Put half the mixture in a blender, together with half of the cream, and blend them together. Tip the purée into a bowl. Repeat for the remainder of the mixture, using the remainder of the cream. Season the creamy purée with the salt and pepper. Chill the soup, and sprinkle with chopped parsley before serving.

CALIFORNIAN ICED FRUIT SOUP

Serves 6

This wine-based fruit soup is spectacular served in a fruit and flower ice bowl. You can make the decorative ice bowl several days in advance for convenience. Set it on a waterproof tray or a deep platter and surround with more flowers and leaves before filling with the fruit soup. The fresh fruit used in the soup can be varied according to seasonal availability.

Ingredients

3 cups fruity white California wine

½ cup sugar, plus more if needed

2 lemons (unwaxed or scrubbed)

3 oranges (unwaxed or scrubbed)

2 ripe peaches, peeled, and sliced, preferably white-fleshed

1½ cups strawberries, halved if large

1 cup blueberries or other small berries

Decorative ice bowl, to serve (see page 187) (optional)

Combine the wine and sugar in a glass or ceramic bowl. Stir to dissolve completely.

Slice the lemons and one of the oranges thinly. Add them to the wine mixture and chill for several hours, stirring occasionally.

Peel and segment the remaining oranges over a bowl to catch the juice. Add the peaches, strawberries, and blueberries, and stir to coat the fruit with orange juice. Taste and add sugar if needed. Cover and chill until serving.

Strain the mixture into a decorative ice bowl or a glass serving bowl and stir in the fruit and accumulated juices. Serve immediately.

LEMON-WINE SOUP

Serves 4

This soup, based on a classic Italian dessert, zabaglione, features the fresh tangy flavor of lemon to balance the sweetness of the wine. The mixture triples in volume, so be sure to use a large bowl.

Ingredients

5 egg yolks

⅓ cup sugar, or more to taste

Rind and juice of 1 medium lemon (unwaxed or scrubbed)

1 cup sweet white wine, such as Muscat or Sauternes

2 cups fresh berries (raspberries, strawberries, or blueberries), hulled or stemmed if necessary, or 2 ripe peaches, pitted, peeled, and sliced

Half-fill a large pan with hot water and set over low heat (do not allow the water to boil). Put the egg yolks, sugar, lemon rind, and juice in a large heatproof bowl which just fits into the pan without touching the water. Set the bowl over the water and, using an electric mixer at low speed or a balloon whisk, beat the mixture, gradually adding the wine. Continue cooking, beating constantly, until it is thick and fluffy, about 10 minutes.

Remove from the heat and continue beating for about 4 minutes until the mixture is cooler.

Chill, covered, until cold. To serve, stir the soup gently, divide among chilled glass bowls and arrange the fruit on top.

PINEAPPLE–MANGO BISQUE

Serves 4

Ingredients

3 Tbsp sugar
2 Tbsp dark rum
2 Tbsp water
3 lb pineapple, peeled, cored, and cut into 1-inch pieces
2 mangoes, peeled, pitted, and cut into ½-inch pieces
3 cups cold milk
A pinch of ground cinnamon
½ cup chilled heavy cream, plus more to serve

In a small pan, combine the sugar, rum, and water. Bring to a boil over high heat and boil until reduced slightly, 1 to 2 minutes. Remove from the heat and set aside to cool.

In a blender or food processor, combine the pineapple, mangoes, and rum syrup with ½ cup milk, and purée until smooth. Strain the soup through a coarse strainer set over a large non-reactive bowl. Whisk in the remaining milk, the cinnamon, and the cream. Cover and leave in the refrigerator until well chilled, 4 to 24 hours.

CHOCOLATE-ORANGE SOUP

Serves 6

This luscious soup is a chocolate lover's dream come true. Use good quality Continental chocolate for the best flavor.

Ingredients

1¼ cups milk
1 vanilla bean
7 oz bittersweet chocolate
3 egg yolks
2 Tbsp sugar
⅞ cup freshly squeezed, strained orange juice
1 Tbsp Cointreau or Grand Marnier
½ cup whipping cream
Chocolate curls to decorate

Put the vanilla bean and milk in a medium pan and bring just to a boil over medium-high heat, stirring frequently. Remove from the heat and cover. Allow to stand for 15 to 20 minutes and remove the vanilla bean.

Break the chocolate into very small pieces and put in a food processor fitted with a steel blade. Process until finely ground.

In a medium bowl, whisk the egg yolks and sugar for 2 to 3 minutes until thick and creamy. Whisk in the hot milk and return the mixture to the pan. With a wooden spoon, stir over medium-low heat until the custard begins to thicken and will coat the back of the spoon (do not allow it to boil or the custard may curdle).

Immediately pour the custard over the chocolate in the food processor and process for 1 minute, or until the chocolate is melted and the mixture is homogenous. Strain into a cold bowl, stir in the orange juice and Cointreau or Grand Marnier and leave to cool, stirring occasionally. When cool, press plastic wrap against the surface and chill until cold.

Divide the chocolate soup among six chilled shallow bowls, swirl some cream in each, and decorate with shaved chocolate curls.

Cook's tip

To make shaved chocolate curls, hold a bittersweet chocolate bar between your hands for a few seconds to soften it slightly. Using a vegetable peeler, scrape along the length of the edge. Chill the chocolate curls until needed for decorating.

SUMMER BERRY SOUP

Serves 4

Croutons in a sweet soup? The combination of the fruit-soaked "croutons" on luscious juicy berries rising from a pool of red berry purée provides a real dose of summer flavor.

Ingredients

1 lb ripe mixed berries (raspberries, blackberries, small strawberries, blueberries, and black currants), hulled or stemmed if necessary

4 Tbsp soft light brown sugar, or to taste

8 slices firm white bread or brioche

6 Tbsp heavy cream

Additional berries and mint leaves, to decorate

For the raspberry purée

12 oz ripe raspberries

6 Tbsp confectioners' sugar, or to taste

Combine the mixed berries and brown sugar in a nonreactive pan and set over medium-low heat until the juices start to run, about 3 to 4 minutes. (The fruit should not be completely cooked.) Remove from the heat and leave to cool slightly. Strain the fruit, without pressing down on it, and reserve the juice in a large bowl.

Line the bottom of four ramekins (about ¾-cup capacity) with rounds of wax paper. Cut eight rounds from the bread the same diameter as the ramekins. Dip four of the bread rounds in the reserved juice and place in the bottom of the ramekins.

Divide the fruit among the four ramekins, pressing it down gently. Dip the remaining bread rounds in the reserved juice and place on top of the fruit. Cover the ramekins tightly and chill for at least 3 hours or overnight.

For the raspberry purée, put the raspberries in a food processor fitted with a steel blade and process until smooth, then press through a strainer. Alternatively, work the berries through the fine blade of a food mill. Add the purée to the reserved juices from the fruit and add the confectioners' sugar, plus more if you wish, and stir until it has dissolved. Cover and chill until cold.

To serve, unmold the ramekins into chilled shallow bowls and remove the paper. Pour the raspberry purée around them and drizzle the cream into the purée. Place a few berries on the top of each serving with mint leaves to decorate.

MELON AND PESTO SOUP

Serves 4

A chilled melon soup that is perfect for summer entertaining as it actually benefits from being made up to a day in advance. It's a marvelous way of using up the shells of melons that you have balled for other dishes.

Ingredients

4 cups Galia melon purée (made from 2 melons)

1 mild green chile, seeded and chopped very fine

⅔ cup water

3 Tbsp best quality pesto sauce

Salt and white pepper

Lime juice, to taste

Blend the melon purée with all the remaining ingredients, adding just enough lime juice to lift the flavor of the soup.

Chill the soup for at least 2 hours, then serve over a little crushed ice. Crisp toasts made with Italian bread and flavored with butter are a perfect accompaniment.

Cook's tip

It is essential to use the very best pesto sauce—it should be slightly sweet, and made just with basil, garlic, Parmesan, and pine nuts.

APRICOT SOUP

Serves 6

This bright, colorful dessert tastes of summer sunshine, even in winter. Using two kinds of apricots intensifies the flavor and you can make the purées up to one day ahead for easy assembly just before serving.

Ingredients

4 oz dried apricots

1 cup orange juice plus more if needed

1 lb fresh apricots, halved and pitted

4 Tbsp sweet white wine

1–2 Tbsp sugar

2 Tbsp apricot or peach liqueur

⅔ cup crème fraîche or sour cream

Combine the dried apricots and orange juice in a nonreactive pan. Set over medium-low heat and simmer, covered, until the apricots are tender, about 35 minutes. Set aside to cool.

Combine the fresh apricots, wine, and sugar to taste in a medium-sized nonreactive pan and bring to a boil. Reduce the heat and simmer until the fruit is very tender, about 25 minutes. Transfer the fruit to a food processor fitted with a steel blade and process until smooth, then press through a strainer into a bowl. Stir in the liqueur and chill until cold.

Scrape the dried apricot mixture into the food processor and process until smooth. Add the crème fraîche or sour cream and pulse just until combined. The mixture should be about the same consistency as the cooked fresh

apricots; add more orange juice if necessary. Transfer to a bowl and chill until cold.

To serve, divide the fresh apricot mixture among chilled bowls and put a large spoonful of the dried apricot and cream mixture in the center, dividing it evenly. Using the handle of a small spoon or a skewer, draw the dried apricot mixture out toward the edge of the bowl in five or six places to make a starburst pattern, curving at the outer edges, if you wish.

Melon and Pesto Soup ▶

GARNISHES AND ACCOMPANIMENTS

Soup embellishments can be anything from sauces to stir in, like rouille, to Parmesan puffs or dumplings, to a simple swirl of cream on top. The idea is to provide visual interest. Some sort of embellishment gives even the simplest soup a real flavor. Garnishes and accompaniments are especially important to complete and enhance the experience when soup is served as the main course.

Bread in one form or another is the most common soup garnish, in fact, the earliest soup was hot liquid poured over bread. Croutons made from bread come in all shapes and sizes, bread crumbs may be the binding for dumplings, and bread itself is sometimes used as a thickener in puréed soups. A simple loaf of crusty bread is often the most satisfying partner to soup.

OTHER EMBELLISHMENTS

Some soups have traditional garnishes without which they seem incomplete. Fish soups in France are often served with garlicky mayonnaise-like sauces—*rouille* and *aïoli*—in addition to croutons. These can give a lift to other kinds of soup as well, such as Chicken Minestrone. These powerful sauces are best in robust soups.

Consommés and clear soups need embellishment and they offer a perfect opportunity to experiment with all sorts of garnishes. You can vary a soup significantly by changing its accompaniment. For example, you could put chicken quenelles in Tarragon Chicken Consommé, as in the recipe, or alternatively, add dumplings, home-made noodles, poached quail eggs, or other things you are likely to have to hand, such as cooked rice, finely diced tomatoes, or thin ribbons of spinach.

SERVING WITH FLAIR

It is difficult to give precise guidelines for anything as individual as creativity and style. Give your imagination free rein. Experiment and don't worry if it doesn't work out perfectly.

Create drama with color contrast. This can be the whiteness of sour cream on deep red borscht or yellow nasturtium blossoms on asparagus soup. Dramatic impact is easier to achieve with contrast.

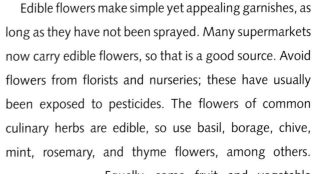

The attraction of most garnishes is the visual element, but a contrast of texture is also appealing. Crispy fried onions or crumbled bacon sprinkled over a creamy soup brings a delightful element of surprise.

Use something in an unexpected way, such as thin ribbons of fresh spinach instead of chopped parsley when an herbal garnish is appropriate, or use sprigs of basil leaves instead of chopped ones.

Select flavors that work together. For example, chive flowers would be better on Sweet Potato and Leek Soup than on Sesame, Carrot, and Parsnip because the chive flavor echoes the leek, both being of the onion family.

Edible flowers make simple yet appealing garnishes, as long as they have not been sprayed. Many supermarkets now carry edible flowers, so that is a good source. Avoid flowers from florists and nurseries; these have usually been exposed to pesticides. The flowers of common culinary herbs are edible, so use basil, borage, chive, mint, rosemary, and thyme flowers, among others.

Equally, some fruit and vegetable blooms make colorful garnishes; try using the flowers of beans, various squashes, or cherries. Not all flowers are safe to eat or use with food, so consult a specialist if you want to be sure.

DECORATIVE ICE BOWL

Flowers, fruit, and leaves glowing through ice formed into a bowl make a stunning presentation for a cold soup. You could use all herbs and herb flowers for a savory cold soup or carry out the theme of a dessert soup by freezing the same fruit in ice. Make sure the ice bowl is large enough to hold what you plan to serve from it.

Ingredients

Crushed ice
2 freezer-safe bowls (preferably tempered glass), at least 4 pt and 5 pt capacities
Ice cubes or ceramic baking beans
A selection of two or three kinds of small edible flowers and other herb flowers and leaves, free of pesticides
A selection of two or three kinds of small fruit, such as blueberries, red currants, raspberries, small strawberries, cherries, grapes, and halved kumquats

Put a layer of crushed ice in the bottom of the larger bowl. Set the smaller bowl inside and weight it down with ice cubes. Drop some flowers and/or flower petals, some leaves, and some fruit into the space between the two bowls. Add some crushed ice to take up some space between the decorative elements and prevent them from floating. Continue filling the space between the bowls with flowers, fruit, leaves, and crushed ice. Pour in cold water to come up to the rim of the larger bowl and freeze until firm.

To unmold, pour warm water into the smaller bowl and lift it out as soon as the ice around it starts to melt. Dip the larger bowl in warm water and turn the ice bowl out. If not using immediately, store it in the freezer.

For serving, set the ice bowl on a napkin on a tray or platter and decorate the base, if wished, with more leaves, flowers, and fruit.

BAKED AND FRIED GARNISHES

CROUTONS

Croutons come in all shapes and sizes, depending on what they are served with, but their crunchy texture always adds interest. Most often, they are simply thin slices of baguette toasted until dry and crisp; these are almost invariably served with French fish soups. Croutons cut from larger diameter loaves, such as those used in classic French Onion Soup to support the cheese that is *gratinéed* on top, are sometimes called *croûtes*. They can also be made from brown bread, cornbread, brioche, or other foods used like bread, such as polenta. Most croutons keep well and are easily made in advance, especially when you have stale French bread on hand.

Makes about 30, serves 6–8

12-inch piece of baguette, about 2 inches in diameter

Preheat a 350°F oven. Cut the bread into slices, ⅜ inch thick.

Place the slices in one layer on a baking sheet and bake for 8 to 10 minutes, turning once, or until golden.

Serve hot or allow to cool completely and store in an airtight container for up to 3 days or freeze, well wrapped. Serve at room temperature or warm before serving.

VARIATIONS

Garlic Croutons

Rub the toasts with a halved garlic clove after baking. For a less intense garlic flavor, brush one side with garlic-infused oil after turning over.

Cubed Croutons

To make cubed croutons, cut crustless slices of firm sandwich bread or rustic country bread into ½-inch cubes. Place in a single layer on a baking sheet and bake in a preheated 325°F oven for about 20 minutes until golden, shaking the pan occasionally.

Fried Croutons

Both sliced and cubed croutons may be fried instead of baked. Heat oil to a depth of about ½ inch in a small frying pan over medium-high heat. When it starts to smoke, add the croutons and fry until golden, stirring cubes or turning slices for even browning. Drain on paper towels and serve warm or at room temperature.

Polenta Croutons

Use polenta, molded in a loaf pan until firm, then sliced thinly and cut in squares or diamonds. Cook as for Fried Croutons.

Crostini

Crostini are essentially croutons with something on them. In Italy, the topping is often olive spread, anchovy paste, minced cooked chicken livers, or cheese. A handy cheese spread for *crostini* is shredded cheese, a little chopped onion, and enough mayonnaise to hold it together spread on croutons and broiled.

CHEESE STRAWS

These rich flaky pastries are perfect to accompany creamy vegetable soups as they provide a contrast of texture and taste.

Makes about 50

1¾ sticks cold sweet butter

1½ cups flour

⅔ cup cold water

½ cup shredded Gruyère or Parmesan cheese, or a combination

1 egg, beaten with 1 tsp water

3–4 Tbsp shredded Parmesan cheese

Cut the butter in 14 pieces and put into the freezer for 30 minutes, or until very firm.

Put the flour into a food processor. Add the butter and pulse three or four times; there should still be big chunks of butter. Run the machine for 5 seconds while pouring the water through the feed tube, then switch off the machine. Turn out the mixture onto a lightly floured cool work surface and gather into a flat ball. If the butter is soft, chill the dough for 30 minutes or longer before proceeding.

Roll out the dough into a long rectangle about 16 x 6 inches. Fold in thirds, bringing one side over to cover the middle, then the other on top of it, like folding a letter. Roll again into a long rectangle and fold again the same way. Chill the dough for 30 minutes.

Roll out the dough into a long rectangle as before, sprinkle with about one third of the cheese, and fold in thirds. Repeat twice, sprinkling the dough each time with one third of the cheese. Chill the dough, well wrapped, for at least 30 minutes or up to 3 days

Preheat a 425°F oven. On a lightly floured cool work surface, roll out the dough to a thickness of ⅜ inch, brush lightly with egg and sprinkle with Parmesan. Using a long sharp knife, cut the dough into long thin sticks about ⅜ inch wide by 3 inches long. Place about 1 inch apart on large non-stick baking sheets and bake for 8 to 10 minutes until they are golden.

PARMESAN PUFFS

These little cheesy cream puffs are wonderful to garnish consommé.

Makes 50–60

½ cup flour

A pinch of salt

A pinch of freshly grated nutmeg

3 eggs

½ cup water

½ stick sweet butter, cut in 6 pieces

2 Tbsp shredded Parmesan cheese

Preheat a 400°F oven. Lightly grease a large baking sheet.

Sift together the flour, salt, and nutmeg. Beat the eggs in a small bowl.

Bring the water and butter to a boil in a small pan. When the butter has melted, remove from the heat and add the dry ingredients. Beat with a wooden spoon until well incorporated.

Set the pan over low heat and cook the mixture for 1 minute to dry it.

Turn off the heat, add about two thirds of the beaten egg, beat thoroughly, then add a little more and beat again. Stir in the cheese.

Spoon the pastry into a piping bag fitted with a ½-inch plain nozzle and pipe the dough on the baking sheet in small mounds about ½ inch in diameter and about 1½ inches apart. Bake for 15 to 18 minutes until the puffs are well browned. Allow to cool.

OTHER GARNISHES

ROUILLE

This sauce, typically served with certain regional fish soups in France, takes its name from the rust color that the pimento, or roasted red pepper, gives it.

Makes about ¾ cup

²/₃ cup soft white bread crumbs

1–2 garlic cloves, chopped fine

1 egg yolk, at room temperature

½ pimento

1 tsp tomato paste

¾ cup extra virgin olive oil

Soak the bread crumbs in warm water and squeeze dry. Put in a food processor with the garlic, egg yolk, pimento, and tomato paste, and purée until smooth. With the machine running, slowly pour the oil through the feed tube, scraping down the sides as needed.

Scrape into a serving dish or storage container. Use immediately.

CRISPY FRIED ONIONS

These crispy onions make an unusual garnish for creamy vegetable soups. Several large shallots may be substituted for the onion.

Makes about 6 servings

1 large red or yellow onion

Olive or peanut oil for frying

Salt for sprinkling (optional)

Cut the onion in half through the stem and remove the root end. Then place cut-side down and slice very thin. Blot the slices on paper towels.

Heat oil to a depth of about ½ inch in a small deep frying pan over medium-high heat until it begins to smoke. Drop in about one third of the onion slices and fry until deep golden brown. Using a slotted spoon, transfer to paper towels and drain.

Cook the remaining onion slices in batches and drain. Sprinkle the onions lightly with salt, if you wish.

INDEX